MAGIC
WITH SCIENCE

MAGIC WITH SCIENCE

Scientific Tricks, Demonstrations, and
Experiments for Home, Classes, Science
Clubs, and Magic Shows

by WALTER B. GIBSON

Illustrated by RIC ESTRADA

LONDON   *COLLINS*   GLASGOW

ISBN 0 00 106146 1
PRINTED AND MADE IN GREAT BRITAIN BY
WM. COLLINS SONS & CO. LTD.
LONDON AND GLASGOW

Contents

6 CONTENTS

Introduction

Since the dawn of civilization, science and magic have been closely linked. Primitive men utilized scientific methods in their daily lives; for the crude tools of the Stone Age, snares devised to trap wild animals, the first implements fashioned from metal, all represented scientific advances. Any discoveries that were easily explained were regarded as natural, but anything of a puzzling nature was assumed to need some special power to control it. That, to a marked degree, represented the dividing line between the scientific and the magical.

Magnetism offers a striking example of this. In ancient times, it was learned that fragments of magnetic ore, called loadstones, would attract iron. A needle stroked with a loadstone would become magnetized and point north. This led to the invention of the mariner's compass, a simple scientific device and a boon to navigation. But from the behaviour of the compass needle grew the legend of a magic mountain in the Far North, so powerfully magnetic that it could draw the iron nails and spikes from approaching ships and leave their wreckage strewn on its shores.

When Columbus sailed to the discovery of America in 1492, his crew noted a variation in the direction of the compass and wanted to turn back, thinking that the needle was bewitched. The real reason was that the compass does not point to the true North, but to the magnetic North. Columbus was enough of a scientist to explain the phenomenon to the satisfaction of the crew, and thus their superstitions were calmed and mutiny was quelled.

But in 1503, when Columbus and his ships were stranded in Jamaica during his last voyage, he played the part of a magician to forestall trouble with the natives. Playing upon their superstitions, Columbus promised to invoke some real black magic upon a specified day, and black it was, for the natives watched in awe as the sun was blotted out at his command. That kept them subdued until relief ships arrived; for they never realized that Columbus had simply predicted an eclipse, which by his calculations was sure to occur on that date.

In the year 1609, an obscure Dutch optician, Johannes Lippershey, was working on some lenses and happened to hold them to the light, when to his amazement, the spire of a distant church was brought to a spot just outside his window. Since Lippershey had a scientific mind, he realized that he had made a new discovery in optics, and he made it public. It was improved upon by the Italian astronomer, Galileo, who developed the telescope from it.

If Lippershey had known less about lenses, he might have mistaken his discovery for something magical and kept the secret to himself. In that case, it might have been many more years before the telescope was invented. Ever since Galileo's time, however, lenses and mirrors have been used in magical illusions which have been presented on the stage, and many surprising optical tricks can be performed in an impromptu fashion, as will be described in later chapters.

Electrical experiments provide a still more remarkable linkage of science and magic. Until as late as the year 1752, the ancient superstition of a wrathful thunder god hurling shafts of lightning from the sky still gripped the public mind. To give it scientific status, a theory was advanced that lightning was generated from the sulphurous and bituminous substances cast up by volcanic eruptions. The odour of ozone, sometimes noted after a lightning stroke, was mistaken for brimstone, furthering the supposition that the volcanic stuff was actually hell fire, cast by the hand of Satan himself.

When Benjamin Franklin flew a specially constructed kite in 1752 and brought electricity down the kite string from the thunder clouds, science scored another triumph over superstition. From that success, Franklin invented the lightning rod, and within a few years, thousands of American houses were equipped with them. Still there were diehards who clung to the old notions, one man even claiming that Franklin's lightning rods were charging the earth with so much electrical substance that severe earthquakes would surely follow!

Along with important advances in science, interest in lesser experiments had grown steadily, for it was from such trifles that great discoveries were made. Franklin was intrigued with such gadgets. In his youth, he carried a purse woven with asbestos, a fireproof substance that was just then coming into vogue. After letting friends try to set fire to it, only to fail, Franklin blandly explained that he carried such a purse so that his money wouldn't burn a hole in his pocket.

With that, Franklin really set the pace for the era of scientific magic that was to follow and expand to its modern proportions. A few years before Franklin flew his famous kite, a French scientist, Jacques Ozanam, produced four volumes which were later translated into English under the the title, *Recreations in Mathematics and Natural Philosophy*. The term "Natural Philosophy" at that time meant "science," and some twenty years later, another French writer, Guyot, published four volumes of *New*

Recreations, which included various electrical experiments originated by Franklin.

Still later, Dr. William Hooper, a London physician, compiled four volumes of *Rational Recreations,* elucidating the principles of Natural Philosophy, by a series of "easy, entertaining, interesting experiments" taken chiefly from Ozanam and Guyot. In a flowery introduction, Dr. Hooper stated, in part:

> "Should we not endeavour to render useful learning not dull, tedious, and disgustful, not rugged and perplexing, but facile, bland, delightful, alluring, captivating? That Philosophy, with his sober garb and solemn aspect, when led by the hand of the sportive nymph Imagination, decked in all the glowing, ever-varying colours of the skies, may gain admittance to the parties of the gay and careless; and while his awful eye restrains the exuberance of her sallies, the beams that dart from her radiant front may play upon his countenance, and dissipate the cloud that too frequently hangs over his brow."

Today, that can all be put in two words: "Have fun." Some of the experiments described by Dr. Hooper are as intriguing now as they were then; and during the two centuries since his *Rational Recreations* were published, hundreds of others have been devised and recorded, many involving principles unknown in Hooper's time. The best of these have been chosen for this volume. Substitute the word "science" for "philosophy" and "magic" for "imagination." The result will be Science Magic.

Ordinary scientific experiments, while instructive, merely bring results that everyone expects. In contrast, feats of magic, while surprising, may require skill and practice to perform. By combining science with magic, surprise is gained with ease, so you can embark upon a career of wizardry at the very first try. You may decide beforehand whether you should present your marvels as scientific experiments or feats of magic—or, for that matter, as both. In any case, choice of items is important, for the following reasons:

From your standpoint, as well as that of your audience, all experiments in Science Magic fall into one of two groups: challenges and mysteries. Their main difference is that a challenge is essentially a puzzle, which must finally be explained to people, as otherwise they may think there is no solution and the experiment will be meaningless. In contrast, a mystery depends upon a trick which enables you to produce a magical effect, without revealing the secret. Such tricks can be performed time and again, with the same baffling results.

The best plan is to begin with experiments of the challenge type as they are often simple and direct. Either you state that you can accomplish something that is seemingly impossible; or you invite someone to try it. When everyone is sure it can't be done, it is up to you to prove it can be. With feats of balance, demonstrations of inertia, or problems of a geometrical nature, once you have completed the experiment, the method is often obvious.

Hence you have baffled your friends only temporarily. The upshot is that they, too, can puzzle people with the same stunts, for which they should duly thank you. Very little practice is needed with most of these challenges, because if you fail at the first try, you keep on, which makes the experiment look more difficult and therefore better. Since such stunts will make you popular, there is no need to worry because you must disclose the methods in order to prove your point. Often, people forget how the stunts were done, or want you to do them again for their friends.

Finally, so many of these diverting challenges are available that you can always add a few new ones on the next occasion. In such demonstrations, there is no need to plan a regular programme. Carry a few needed items with you and borrow the others as required. Occasionally you can combine one experiment with another, or use one as a follow-up, as will be suggested with the descriptions of certain items. But generally speaking, challenges are individual items in themselves and are most effective when shown in an off-hand manner, so no set routine is necessary.

After puzzling your friends with challenges, you can proceed to baffle them with experiments of the mystery type. You will still be depending on scientific factors, but in this case, the principle is concealed. Many optical tricks are of this type, as are those involving static electricity, magnetism, and pretended hypnotism. Since observers do not know the secret of such a trick, they may credit you with great skill, though actually you are fooling them scientifically. Inject a few of these mysteries into your usual run of challenges and watch how people go for them!

As a rule, you should never divulge the secrets of such tricks as that may spoil future fun. If you have to admit that someone has guessed right, do it with a smile and go on to something else. Remember that you are a scientist as much as a magician. By making that clear at the start, you may save yourself some embarrassing moments if a trick fails.

Even the Great Houdini occasionally took this way out of a dilemma. He once performed with a remarkable "Flying Lamp" that vanished instantly from one table and appeared just as suddenly upon another. Houdini bought the trick from a German magical manufacturer named Conradi, and though it was a marvel of mechanical ingenuity, there were times when it went wrong and reappeared too late, or even worse, too soon. So Houdini used to say: "This trick was invented by a magician named Conradi, and I improved it. If it works, you will know it's my trick. If it doesn't work, it's still Conradi's."

You can use a few quips of your own when an experiment fails, such as, "I forgot to use the magic word for that trick." Or, "The magic word for that one was 'Abracadabra' but I should have said it backwards. Let's try again." Or, "I shouldn't have tried that experiment. I just remembered that it only works when the moon is full." All that adds to the fun.

Gradually, as you use more and more mysteries as opposed to challenges, you can stress tricks rather than puzzles and build a programme that will be almost completely magic. That is when you should make sure that all the required items are available and carry your own, rather than trust to luck. Often, an article used in one trick will do for the next, so that you can move smoothly from one experiment to another.

Even better, as you build up your act, you will find that you can set the stage beforehand, with such items as bottles, glasses, candles, rubber balloons, and other articles all on display. This will intrigue your audience and enable you to pick each item as needed. After finishing each trick, you can put its equipment away in a large box or special case that you have ready for that purpose. This will enable you to dispose of certain articles that might give away the secret if people had a chance to examine them after the trick is finished.

Rehearsal and routining will help as your experiments veer from the purely scientific and take on the aspect of a full-fledged magic show. But no matter how mystifying your performance may become, it is still good policy to inject a few challenges into the act. Letting people worry over a puzzle and then showing them the solution is the best way of adding audience participation to your performance. Also, by showing them a few scientific stunts that they can do, you can politely decline to give them explanations of the more mysterious effects that you prefer to reserve for your very own.

All the experiments that follow have been chosen for definite reasons. First, all items required are either easy to obtain, or are inexpensive. Next, cumbersome experiments demanding too much preparation have been avoided. The few that require the lighting of a match or a candle, or the use of a knife, should be presented with due care and always with an adult present, when performing for children.

MAGIC WITH SCIENCE

Physitrix

Tricks Involving
Various Principles of Physics

Mystic Comeback

- **EFFECT:** A large cake tin is set on its side and rolled along the floor, like a wheel. Soon it stops, then mysteriously reverses itself and rolls back the other way.
- **MATERIALS:** A cake or cookie tin, $3\frac{1}{2}$ inches high and 10 inches in diameter, or approximately those dimensions. A horseshoe magnet, an ounce or more in weight; or any metal weight and some adhesive tape.
- **WHAT TO DO:** Attach the magnet to the inner side of the cake tin and put the cover on the tin. The magnet stays of its own accord unless the tin is non-magnetic. In that case, any metal weight—such as a bolt or nut—can be fixed in place with adhesive tape. All is then ready for the demonstration that follows

Set the tin on its side with the weight near

the top and give it just enough of a forward roll so that it carries past the bottom and almost to the top again. There, it will stop and roll back the other way.

- **WHAT HAPPENS:** If you set the tin with the weight near the top but slightly toward you, it will automatically roll in your direction as the centre of gravity lowers itself. By rolling it one way in the manner described, you put the weight in the exact position for the reverse roll. The forward roll loses its impetus and the backward roll takes control as it normally would have, if this had been presented as a scientific experiment at the start.

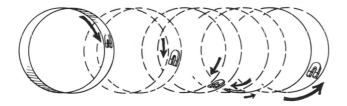

Pillars of Hercules

- **EFFECT:** To prove that a sheet of paper is quite fragile, it is curved slightly, set on edge, and then crumpled with a lazy downstroke of the hand. But you can still set such pieces of paper edgewise and have them support a weight of several pounds.
- **MATERIALS:** Four sheets of fairly small paper, some mending tape or rubber bands, and several good-sized books.
- **WHAT TO DO:** Roll each sheet of paper in-

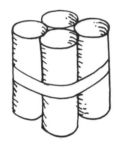

Rubber Band or Adhesive Tape

Strong Paper

• **EFFECT:** A single sheet of paper is laid across two drinking glasses with a wide space between. A third glass is set on the open stretch, and the paper naturally caves downward. But in repeating the experiment, with a certain modification, the paper is shown to be strong enough to support the weight of the glass.

• **MATERIALS:** A sheet of paper and three glasses.

• **WHAT TO DO:** First, lay the paper across two glasses and show that it can't support a third. Then pleat the paper lengthwise, folding one edge ½-inch forward, then doubling it ½-inch back, then forward, backward, and so on, until the entire sheet has

to a tube one inch or more in diameter and either tape it together or gird it with a rubber band. Set these tubes upright as the corners of an imaginary rectangle. Rest a book flat on these "Pillars of Hercules," as you can term them, and when it is set in place, add another book on top, then another and perhaps still more. The paper pillars will support them all.

• **WHAT HAPPENS:** This is a scientific test of simple longitudinal stress, where a short pillar is compressed by opposite forces applied at its ends. The paper pillars serve like hollow metal posts as long as the pressure is straight downward; in fact, the books might as well be resting on a stack of paper sheets. But any strain from another angle will result in compound stress, causing a pillar to collapse, as can be tested by adding too many books.

been pleated. Place it across the two glasses and you can safely set the third on the space between.

• **WHAT HAPPENS:** In pleating, the paper sheet is formed into a series of upright segments, which, when compressed together, become a solid support. In spreading into a zigzag formation, they still retain sufficient strength to withstand a simple downward stress, provided there are enough pleats to keep the formation from becoming too wide.

This is why corrugated metal can stand greater stress or strain than a flat sheet of metal. The experiment simply applies the principle to paper.

Bottle and Straw

• **EFFECT:** A drinking straw is inserted in an empty soda water bottle and immediately the bottle is lifted by the straw.

• **MATERIALS:** A few straws and an empty bottle.

• **WHAT TO DO:** Bend the straw a few inches from one end and insert this end well down in the bottle. Lift the upper end slowly and the bent straw will bring the bottle with it.

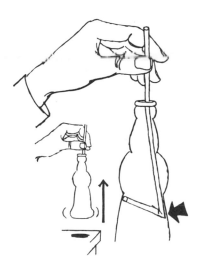

• **WHAT HAPPENS:** The bent portion of the straw wedges at a cross-angle, thus serving as a brace. The curvature of the longer portion brings the centre of gravity directly under the point of suspension, thus completing the requirements for the experiment. Tests with several straws may be necessary to ensure success.

Comeback Ball

• **EFFECT:** A small ball is rolled along a table from hand to hand. Finally, it is given a short roll in which it stops halfway and then whizzes backward entirely of its own accord.

• **MATERIALS:** Almost any small ball ranging in weight from a ping-pong ball to a golf ball.

• **WHAT TO DO:** Roll the ball easily a few

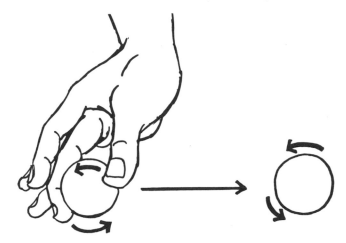

times, from the right hand to the left. Then hold it in the right hand, thumb above, second finger below, with the knuckle of the finger close to the table. Give the hand a slight jerk toward the left, and at the same time, snap the thumb and fingers in opposite directions. The ball will travel along the table toward the left, stop and scoot back to the right in a most surprising fashion.

• **WHAT HAPPENS:** The jerk sends the ball forward along the table although the snap of the fingers spins it backward, or toward the right. The ball appears to roll forward —or to the left—but it really slides. Once that motion is counteracted by the spin, the ball rolls the other way.

• **REMARKS:** Different techniques are needed with balls of different weight, and sidewise or angled spins are also possible. A good forward slide and back spin give the effect of an automobile wheel coming out of a skid and starting off as its tyre tread takes hold.

Mystic Rising Card

• **EFFECT:** A playing card is chosen from a pack and pushed down into a drinking glass, which is then covered by the pack, imprisoning the chosen card. The pack is then lifted and given a sharp snap. At that command, the chosen card rises of its own accord, even toppling from the glass.

• **MATERIALS:** A fairly tall glass, slightly wider than a playing card, at the top, but considerably narrower at the bottom. A pack of fairly new playing cards with a glossy or plastic finish, so the edges are quite smooth. A small piece of dry soap.

• **WHAT TO DO:** Rub the inner walls of the glass with soap, which can then be spread with the fingertips so that it becomes a thin film which is no longer discernible. Have this glass ready with the pack.

• **WHAT HAPPENS:** When a card is chosen and pushed down into the glass, its lower

end, being pliable, tends to spread with the mechanical action of a spring. This would force the card upward, except for the slight friction from the gradually widening sides of the glass, but that, in turn, is counteracted by the application of the soap, which acts as a lubricant. The weight of the pack prevents the card from rising too soon, but once it is removed, the experiment goes into automatic action. The quick snap given to the pack is simply byplay to make the rising of the card seem more magical.

• **REMARKS:** Many types of drinking glasses are suitable for this experiment, so several varieties should be tested to find the best. A duplicate glass should be kept handy, so that the soaped glass can be laid aside after the trick and the duplicate used in a later experiment. Anyone trying to make a card rise from the untreated glass will be disappointed.

Piercing a Potato

• **EFFECT:** An ordinary drinking straw is held in one hand and a potato in the other. With a forward thrust, the straw is driven straight through the potato, piercing it completely. Yet, when the straw is withdrawn, it can be bent and folded to prove that it is quite ordinary.

• **MATERIALS:** A raw potato of average size and a common drinking straw.

• **WHAT TO DO:** Both the potato and the straw can be given for examination beforehand, but when the straw is returned, it is taken at the far end between the right thumb and fingers. The potato is then poised in the left hand, while the right thumb secretly bends the end of the straw inward and flattens it against the fingers, keeping it firmly pressed there. All that remains is to give the straw a straight, direct thrust against the

end strips and tear them in oppposite directions at the same time, so that the centre strip will fall entirely clear. Strangely, whoever tries it is sure to fail.

• **MATERIALS:** Several fair-sized pieces of newspaper.

• **WHAT TO DO:** Make two preliminary tears as described, leaving about two inches still to be torn in each case. In tearing, a person will find that one tear invariably gives way, leaving the other intact. Always, one end piece will come free; never both.

side of the potato, and it will continue on through. In withdrawing the straw, the right thumb straightens the end, so that it appears ordinary; but it is a good plan to give the straw a few folds later on, so that no one will suspect anything.

• **WHAT HAPPENS:** By sealing the far end of the straw, no air can escape when the near end is driven squarely into the potato. The air, being compressed by the thrust, acts as interior rod or pillar, strengthening the straw sufficiently to insure the penetration.

• **WHAT HAPPENS:** There is sure to be difference in the original tears, such as their length, their direction, or the weakness of the paper fibres at a particular point. As a result, one always gives way before the other, and you prove conclusively that this simplest of experiments is so difficult it can't be done.

Tearing the Paper

• **EFFECT:** A piece of newspaper is torn part way through in two places, forming a row of three strips. Anyone is invited to take the

The Restored Match

• **EFFECT:** A large match is wrapped in the centre of a handkerchief. Through the cloth, the match is deliberately broken into three parts. Yet when the handkerchief is unfolded, the match drops on the table, completely restored.

• **MATERIALS:** A match and a plain handkerchief.

• **WHAT TO DO:** Fold the match in the centre of the handkerchief, show its shape through the cloth, and actually break it with your thumbs and forefingers, about one-third of the way from one end. Then move along and repeat the breaking process near the other end. Now, gather the centre folds more tightly and as you do, carefully straighten the broken portions of the match through the cloth. Take the handkerchief by one cor-

SNAP!

SNAP under cover

• **WHAT HAPPENS:** Here, the pliability of wood fibres plays the vital part. When the match is broken with a sharp snap, its sections bend inward, with the innermost fibres remaining intact and acting like a hinge. By pressing the segments outward, the hinged portion will guide them back into place so that the broken fibres will mesh. Thus the match is straightened and shown apparently restored.

• **REMARKS:** This can be tested without using a handkerchief, in order to note the scientific principle upon which the experiment depends. To break a match fully, it must be snapped one way, then the other. A single snap is not sufficient, but that fact is concealed by breaking the match inside the handkerchief.

Sharp SNAP

When pressing segments

Pliable inner fibres, still intact, act as HINGES!

ner, shake it slightly and the match will drop on the table, apparently restored.

An Animated Hairpin

• **EFFECT:** A hairpin is set astride a ruler which is held so that the ends of the hairpin touch the table. At command, the hairpin walks along the ruler, forward and backward, in a manner which is not only lifelike, but uncanny.

• **MATERIALS:** A large hairpin and a ruler, preferably of the 12-inch type.

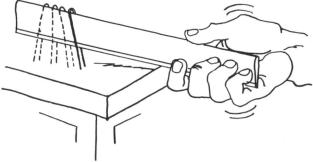

• **WHAT TO DO:** Set the hairpin on the ruler and hold the near end of the ruler level, but just clear of the table, gripping it in your fist. When you lower the ends of the hairpin to the table, you will find that the hairpin, if leaning slightly forward, will automatically walk away from you. By raising the ruler, then lowering it so the hairpin leans backward, the hairpin will walk toward you of its own accord. Just the slightest of tilts will speed up the pace.

• **WHAT HAPPENS:** The muscular vibration of your hand supplies the motive power for the animated hairpin. Since your hand is not resting on the table, it is impossible to keep it absolutely steady. Imperceptible though your muscular reaction may be, it makes the hairpin walk forward and backward, according to its tilt.

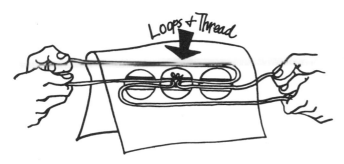

Grandmother's Necklace

• **EFFECT:** Three wooden beads are strung on a pair of strings. The strings are crossed and one pair is given to a person on the left; the other pair is given to someone on the right. The beads are covered with a handkerchief and beneath the cloth, they are mysteriously removed from the strings, which are drawn tight by the surprised spectators.

• **MATERIALS:** Three wooden beads with holes drilled through their centres. Small

wooden blocks can be used instead. Two pieces of soft white string, exactly alike and about two feet long. A bit of white thread.

• **WHAT TO DO:** Tie the thread about the centre of the strings, which are laid together evenly. This enables you to bend back the ends of the strings, so they become two loops, joined at the centre by the thread. Run them through the beads, so that the looped centre is concealed within the middle bead.

Exhibited thus, the two strings appear to run straight through the beads in normal fashion. But when each person is given two opposite ends and the strings are pulled, the thread breaks, the beads drop off and the handkerchief is removed to show the strings as good as ever.

• **WHAT HAPPENS:** The beads naturally drop because only the thread sustains them. But the switch of the ends actually gives each person an end of each string, so they finish with the strings exactly as they were originally supposed to be.

• **REMARKS:** This is one of the oldest experiments in scientific magic, dating back to the jugglery of the Middle Ages, and from it have derived more intricate tricks that are still popular today.

Name the Date

• **EFFECT:** Several pennies, all alike except for their dates, are lying on a plate. While the performer's back is turned, a person is told to take one of the coins and dump the rest into a hat. The chosen coin is then passed to all persons present, so that each can note the date and remember it. That done, it is tossed into the hat and shaken up with the rest of the coins. Yet the performer, reaching into the hat and bringing coins out one by one, stops when he comes to the right coin, looks at it, and names the date, which everyone confirms.

• **MATERIALS:** Several pennies with different dates. A cold plate. A borrowed hat.

Cold Plate

Borrowed Hat

Pennies with different Dates

When passed around coin absorbs HEAT from Hands..

The WARM COIN IS The One!

Cold Coins

• **WHAT TO DO:** Have the coins spread on the plate so everyone can see how similar they are. Turn your back and tell someone to take a coin and immediately pour the rest into the hat, directly from the plate. Add that you want everyone to note the date on the chosen coin, as the more persons thinking of it, the better your chance of naming it. After the chosen coin is dropped into the hat, pick out the coins one by one. You will note that all feel cold, except one. The warm one will be the chosen coin.

• **WHAT HAPPENS:** Metal normally becomes

cold, particularly when kept in contact with anything like a cold plate. But when a coin is handled, it absorbs heat from the human hands. By insisting that everyone look at the date, the coin is passed around sufficiently for you to distinguish its warmth the moment you touch it.

Blocks and Rings

• **EFFECT:** Three wooden blocks are shown on two strings which run through holes in the centres of the blocks. The ends of the strings are crossed and a pair of finger rings are strung on each pair of ends. People hold the ends of the strings, and the blocks and rings are covered with a handkerchief. When the ends are pulled, the blocks fall from the strings, but the rings mysteriously remain in place.

• **MATERIALS:** Three blocks with holes drilled through their centres. Two finger rings which may be borrowed. Two pieces of identical string, a short thread, and a handkerchief.

• **WHAT TO DO:** Prepare the strings as with "Grandmother's Necklace," (see page 23) bending back the ends and running them through the holes in the blocks so that the doubled centre is hidden within the middle block. Cross the strings, but before giving them to anyone, slide a ring over each pair of ends. Let people hold the ends and pull as soon as the handkerchief covers the blocks and rings. The thread breaks, releasing the blocks, but the rings remain on the strings.

• **WHAT HAPPENS:** The blocks fall from the broken centre, but the rings stay because they were not put on the strings until after the ends were crossed. That made them two straight strings—exactly what people took them to be—so far as the rings were concerned.

• **REMARKS:** If either "Grandmother's Necklace" or the "Blocks and Rings" are set up beforehand, the strings can simply be doubled and inserted in the middle bead or block, without using a thread as a link. But with the thread, it is possible to conceal the centre between the thumb and fingers of one hand, while openly threading the strings with the other hand.

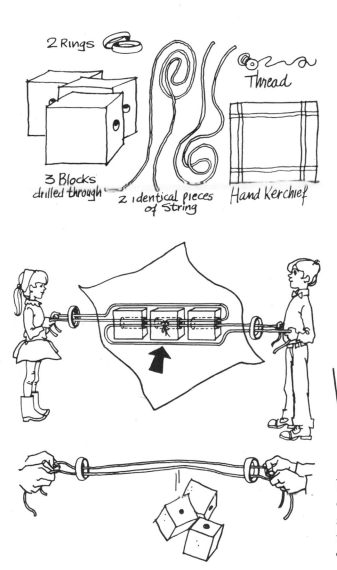

The Marked Match

• **EFFECT:** Several large wooden matches are examined and found to be absolutely identical. One match is then marked with four short pencil lines along each side, so lightly that it would be impossible to feel the marks. The performer then places his hands beneath the table, where he is given the matches, one

by one. He passes each one back until he receives the marked match. Though he has absolutely no chance to see it, he announces that it is the marked match—and he is right!

• **MATERIALS:** A dozen wooden matches. A

pencil. Two pairs of steel pliers. Some bits of paper.

• **WHAT TO DO:** Prepare one match by wrapping bits of paper around its ends; then grip the ends with the pliers. With one hand, twist an end of the match slightly forward, with the other hand twist the opposite end slightly backward. Continue this action with the pliers until the match will yield when tested with the thumbs and fingers alone.

Have the flexible match with the others when you present the experiment. Mark it with the pencil and let people examine the marked match with the rest. Whatever else they do, they will never think of twisting the ends in opposite directions, rotary fashion. But you think of it, when the matches are handed to you beneath the table. The one that gives when you apply the right twist will be the marked match, every time.

• **WHAT HAPPENS:** From the scientific standpoint, this is one of the most ingenious of magical experiments. Here, you take advantage of the fact that wood fibres weaken under continued strain. You are dealing with torsion instead of just pliability, for if you bend the matches slightly, as though to break them, you will find no perceptible difference between the marked match and the others.

All this is important scientifically, for it explains why unexpected accidents may happen, even though supposedly thorough precautions have been taken. Metals, too, can weaken as the result of fatigue, as in the case of aeroplane wings or the cables of suspension bridges.

The Perpetual Propeller

• **EFFECT:** A two-bladed propeller cut from cardboard is tacked to the end of a notched stick. When the stick is rubbed rapidly, the propeller starts to whirl and keeps on going as if impelled by some perpetual force.

• **MATERIALS:** A cardboard propeller, a tack, and a piece of dowel or a similar stick, with a series of notches cut at regular intervals.

• **WHAT TO DO:** Hold the end of the stick with your left thumb and fingers. Double your right fingers and run your extended right thumb along the notches. A quick, repeated action will start the propeller spinning and it will continue as long as the same motion is applied.

• **WHAT HAPPENS:** Due to the notches, the motion of the right thumb and fingers veers from a straight line and causes the stick to rotate very slightly. The rotation is transmitted to the improvised propeller which revolves accordingly. By reversing the rubbing process, the propeller can be spun in the opposite direction. When whirling at full speed, the effect is highly baffling.

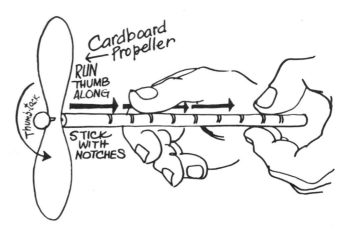

The Rising Tube

• **EFFECT:** A long cardboard tube is shown threaded on a still longer string. One end of the string is held upward, and the tube is allowed to slide downward to the other hand. There is nothing phenomenal yet, but wait! At the word "Rise!" the tube mysteriously ascends the string almost to the top. It repeats this, falling and rising, as often as desired.

• **MATERIALS:** A cardboard mailing tube, 18 inches long, 1¼ inches in diameter. A string, 36 inches in length. Another string, 22 inches in length. (All dimensions approximate.) A small curtain ring of less diameter than the tube. A thumbtack.

• **WHAT TO DO:** Tie the ring to one end of the short string and drop it down through the tube, so it just barely emerges at the lower end. Lay the tube flat and push the thumbtack just inside the lower rim of the tube, so that the tack points outward. Tie one end of the long string around the head of the thumbtack. Push the other end of the

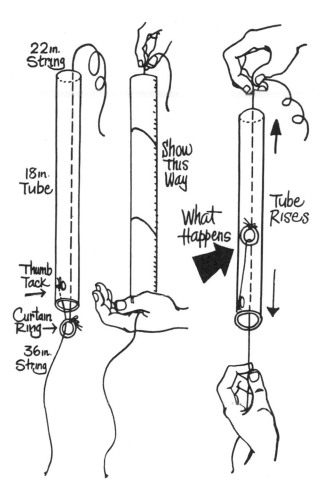

22 in. String
18 in. Tube
Thumb Tack →
Curtain Ring →
36 in. String
Show This Way
What Happens
Tube Rises

long string as far through the ring as it will go.

Now, take the end of the short string at the top of the tube and draw it upward until the ring is hidden inside the lower end of the tube. Hold the end of the short string with your right hand and take the free end of the long string with your left hand. Draw the ends of the strings taut, then lift the tube upright, your right hand above, your left hand below.

You will find that the tube hangs steadily near the top of what appears to be a single string more than twice the length of the tube. This is the way you show the tube and string to start, so it is a good plan to grip the top of the tube by bending one or two fingers inward and pressing the rim of the tube against the right palm, as if you were holding the tube in place.

Relax the left hand's hold on the lower end of the supposedly single string and the tube will slide down nearly to the bottom as it presumably should. Then pull the ends strongly and the tube will rise to the top, apparently of its own accord. It can be made to fall and rise as often as you want; and it can be stopped halfway by simply keeping the strings taut instead of pulling them or relaxing the lower end.

• **WHAT HAPPENS:** It is a simple illustration of the pulley principle, with the long string hoisting the tube, just as pulling the end of a doubled rope raises a weight on the other end. If done openly, there would be no mystery, but the tube conceals the block-and-tackle arrangement which is responsible for the lift. Here, science is strongly applied to create a baffling illusion.

• **REMARKS:** The supposedly single string becomes shorter each time the tube is raised, and it lengthens whenever the tube is lowered. This, however, is not noticed, due to the length of the tube itself. A shorter tube can be used, with the strings proportionately shorter, but the extent of the rise necessarily will be reduced and the experiment will be less effective.

Seesaw Sorcery

• **EFFECT:** A ruler is laid across a pencil, and two paper cups partly filled with water are balanced on opposite sides, like a seesaw. Without touching either of the cups or the ruler—or even the pencil—you make the the cups seesaw up and down.

• **MATERIALS:** Two paper cups, some water, a pencil, and a ruler.

• **WHAT TO DO:** Pour water into each cup, until each is more than two-thirds full and both balance nicely. Dip your right forefinger in one cup and that side will go downward.

Dip your left forefinger in the other cup and lift your right finger; down goes the left side. By alternating your fingers in this fashion, you can keep the seesaw going back and forth, without ever touching cups or ruler.

• **WHAT HAPPENS:** Dipping an object into a

cup of water increases the weight according to the amount of water displaced. An ancient Greek named Archimedes discovered this while taking a bath and you can prove it today by simply demonstrating the seesaw cups.

Ups and Downs

• **EFFECT:** Two empty paper cups teeter on the ends of a ruler whenever you dip a finger into one; yet you never touch the cups.

• **MATERIALS:** Two paper cups, a ruler, and a pencil.

• **WHAT TO DO:** Balance the ruler across the

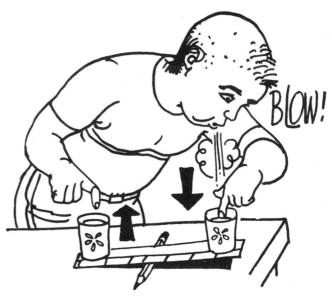

the pencil, with the cups on opposite sides. As you dip a finger into a cup, lean in that direction and blow downward into the cup. Do the same with the other cup and you can keep them going up and down as long as you want.

• **WHAT HAPPENS:** The cups are so light that a mere breath can disturb their equilibrium. Being open, they catch a puff of wind like little sails. Hence it is easy to blow so gently that the action will not be detected.

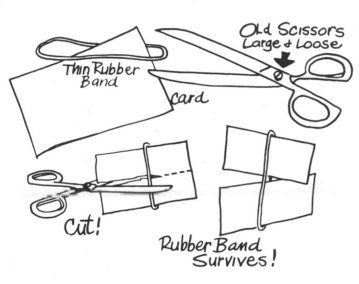

Snappy

• **EFFECT:** A rubber band is put around a calling card or any piece of thin cardboard of suitable size. The card is cut in half with a pair of scissors, squarely across the rubber band. Yet the rubber band is uninjured and can be snapped back and forth to prove it.

• **MATERIALS:** A fairly thin rubber band and a thin card just wide enough for the rubber band to be girded about it and kept taut. A pair of old scissors, which must be large and loose.

• **WHAT TO DO:** Put the rubber band around the card and cut straight through the card, directly across the rubber band. A long, care-ful cut will sever the card, leaving the rubber band intact. If you have trouble finishing the cut, start from one edge and go as far as the rubber band. Then turn the card around and cut from the other edge so that the cuts meet soon after the scissor blades pass the rubber band. People will still be puzzled by the survival of the rubber band.

• **WHAT HAPPENS:** The card, being stiff, is easily cut, while the rubber band, being pliable, is squeezed down between the loose blades of the scissors. Thus two simple scientific principles of cutting are at work, each producing an opposite result. This should be tested beforehand, to make sure the scissors are neither too sharp nor too dull; too tight nor too loose.

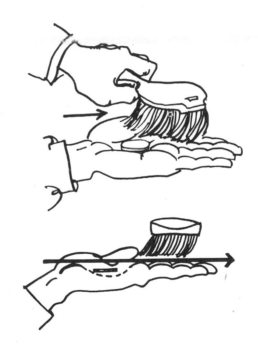

Brush it Away

• **EFFECT:** A penny is laid in the palm of your hand and you give someone a hairbrush, telling him to sweep away the coin. To his surprise, he is unable to do so.

• MATERIALS: A coin and a brush.

• WHAT TO DO: Lay the coin in your hand as described, but tell the person that he must try to brush it away in long, straight sweeps. He can't succeed because the brush will ride over the coin without contacting it.

• WHAT HAPPENS: The coin rests in the hollow of your palm, which is much deeper than most persons realize. The brush is too wide to dip down into the hollow, hence it misses the coin entirely.

The Bouncing Cork

• EFFECT: A person is given an ordinary cork and asked to drop it on the table so it stands on end. Always, the cork bounces when it

hits and lands on its side; that is, until you try it. Then it stands on end.

• MATERIALS: A cork, with a table handy.

• WHAT TO DO: Drop the cork so it hits on its side. It will bounce, of course, but with a little practice you can gauge the drop so it finishes standing upright.

• WHAT HAPPENS: Due to its lightness and resiliency, the cork will bounce no matter how it is dropped. Landing on its side, it will often bounce on end; and the bounce being much less forceful than the drop, the cork can stay balanced on end. Test this beforehand to specify the distance of the drop, which in turn governs the force of the bounce.

Cut and Restored String

• EFFECT: A length of string is cut in half with a pair of scissors, and both sections are shown separately. The ends of the string are brought together and it is allowed to drop from one end. The string promptly dangles in a single length, restored to its original form.

• MATERIALS: A piece of yarn, 12 inches or more in length. A pair of scissors or a knife.

• WHAT TO DO: Show the yarn, but call it "a piece of string." Cut it near the centre, show the two pieces and bring the cut ends together between the thumb and fingers of your left hand. Gather the two dangling ends with your right thumb and fingers, so that the ends overlap an inch or so.

As you bring those lower ends upward, roll them together, at the same time raising your left hand and remarking, "Here we have the two cut ends, so I'll put the other ends with them, making four ends in all." Bring the hands together, move them up and down, then hold one cut end and let the other fall. The string will dangle freely, apparently restored to a single piece.

• **WHAT HAPPENS:** Since the supposed string is actually yarn, its fibres are fluffy and adhere closely when the ends are rolled together. Be sure to use yarn with a loose twist and test it beforehand. Keep the dangling "string" slightly in motion and no one will notice the slight thickness near its centre. At the finish, you can gather it together and put it in your pocket without any chance of its coming apart.

Optrix

Tricks and Illusions
Involving Optical Principles

Wine to Water

- **EFFECT:** A small glass is shown filled with dark, purplish wine. It is covered with a handkerchief and changes to a light red wine. Covered again, it becomes water, which anyone may drink.
- **MATERIALS:** A small glass, preferably the type with a stem. Two thin but stiff pieces of celluloid or plastic, one red, the other blue or green. These are cut to fit the glass exactly; this can be done neatly by using a piece of stiff paper for a pattern. Some water, a handkerchief and an object to serve for a stand, such as a book or a box.
- **WHAT TO DO:** Beforehand fill the glass and insert the plastic cut-outs together, so that when they are viewed broadside, the water will appear to be dark wine. Set the glass on

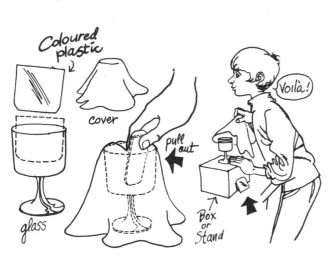

a box and cover it with the handkerchief until you are ready to perform the experiment.

Then lift the handkerchief and state that you have a glass filled with dark wine, as everyone can see. Cover it momentarily and in lifting the handkerchief, insert your thumb and forefinger behind the hem and bring away one cut-out, leaving only the red. Drop the cut-out behind your improvised stand.

Now you have what appears to be a light red wine. Cover the glass completely with the handkerchief and this time lift the red cut-out through the cloth itself. Drop the handkerchief, pick up the glass and show that it is water, nothing else!

- **WHAT HAPPENS:** Without the water, the cut-outs would look like what they really are. But once the water has been poured into the glass, the colours are diffused due to the refraction, and they create the illusion that the liquid itself is coloured.

Red, combined with either green or blue, creates a colour resembling dark wine; the red alone, appears as wine of a reddish hue. Simply be careful never to show the glass with cut-outs edgewise toward the onlookers, or the illusion will be dispelled.

- **REMARKS:** This is an excellent stunt to include in an exhibition of "Chemical Magic" as the spectators, after witnessing actual chemical changes, will be really puzzled by this one.

The Bending Pencil

- **EFFECT:** A pencil is held horizontally by one end, gripped between the thumb and fingers of the right hand. The hand begins an up-and-down motion and the pencil begins to wiggle, as though made of rubber. Yet it proves to be an ordinary wooden pencil.
- **MATERIALS:** A fairly long pencil.
- **WHAT TO DO:** Hold the tip of the pencil between thumb and forefinger; keep it level and make short, quick, up-and-down motions. Watch the pencil and when it seems to wiggle, you will know that you are doing it right.
- **WHAT HAPPENS:** When you move an object rapidly up and down, it produces a blurred effect. With a wheel and other moving objects, this follows a normal pattern, even though it is an optical illusion. But in the

case of the "bending pencil," the far end is covering a much greater distance than the near end, with its short, jerky action. The result is a double illusion of a slight bend and a greater one, so the pencil itself looks pliable.
- **REMARKS:** Some novelty dealers sell imitation pencils made of rubber that really will bend when people try to write with them. With such a pencil, you can do the "wiggle trick" and then show everyone that it worked because the pencil was made of rubber. Then, repeat it with a wooden pencil and they will be all the more surprised.

The Mixed-up Mirror

- **EFFECT:** Two words are printed on a card and held in front of a mirror. Everyone knows that the letters should be reflected in reverse, but in this case, it doesn't hold true. One word remains exactly as it was, though letters in the other are turned about.

- **MATERIALS:** A card, a pencil, and a mirror.
- **WHAT TO DO:** Print the words CHOICE QUALITY on the card and turn it upside down as you hold it before the mirror. The first word will still read CHOICE, but QUALITY will have most of its letters topsy-turvy and two of them (Q and L) reversed.
- **WHAT HAPPENS:** The optical law of reversed mirror writing works as usual, but a careful study will show that the letters H, O, and I are the same backward, forward or upside down; while C and E, when inverted, assume their regular appearance in a mirror. If people fail to notice that the card is turned upside down in front of the mirror, they will be doubly mystified.

The Mysterious Rod

• **EFFECT:** Two words are printed on a card and viewed through a glass or plastic rod. One stays the same; the other turns upside down and backward.

• **MATERIALS:** A card, a pencil, and a glass or plastic rod.

• **WHAT TO DO:** Use the CHOICE QUALITY card and the result will be the same as with a mirror. CHOICE stays as it is, while QUALITY takes on a mixed appearance.

• **WHAT HAPPENS:** Due to refraction, the curved surface of the transparent rod inverts whatever is viewed through it. Thus CHOICE apparently remains the same, while QUALITY is inverted and some of its letters are backward.

The Penetrating Rod

• **EFFECT:** A short, rounded wooden rod is impaled on the loose bar of a large blanket pin, which is then closed. The rod is then brought around until it is blocked by the solid bar of the pin. With a stroke of the finger, the rod is apparently knocked right through the solid bar. This amazing feat is repeated time after time with the same baffling result.

• **MATERIALS:** A large blanket pin; a small-size dowel from 3 to 4 inches in length, with a small hole bored crosswise through the centre.

• **WHAT TO DO:** Impale the dowel on the free rod of the pin, and close it. Hold the pin horizontally with the left thumb and fore-finger at either end, but with the solid bar on the near side. With the right forefinger push the far end of the rod around until it comes up beneath the solid pin.

Now comes the amazing part. Bring the right forefinger up beneath that same end of the rod, giving it a hard, upward flip. You, yourself, will be nonplussed to see the wooden rod come right up through the solid bar. Swing it around and snap it up through again. If you do it right, you just won't believe it happened, it is that good. But it does happen, though differently than most observers suppose.

• **WHAT HAPPENS:** The hard upward snap causes the rod to bounce back in the oppo-

site direction, so that instead of coming up through the steel bar—which is utterly impossible—it flies around the other way and comes downward and frontward so rapidly that it actually seems to come up through. The result is a most remarkable illusion of the rare type where quickness actually deceives the eye.

• REMARKS: Repetition makes this all the more wonderful, once the knack of snapping the rod is acquired. Even a false flip will not injure the illusion, but will simply pass as a time the "penetration" did not occur. But the better the knack, the stronger the effect.

To test this "penetration," take a large kitchen match, break off the head, and impale the matchstick on the loose end of a large safety pin. It may take a few trials to find a matchstick that will work effectively, but when it does, the result is quite as good. So the matchstick version makes an excellent model for the larger device.

Card Vanishes from Glass

• EFFECT: Several playing cards are placed beneath a handkerchief, and one card is drawn away through the cloth. Still covered, the card is pushed down into a tall drinking glass. The handkerchief is whipped away and the card has vanished from the glass.

• MATERIALS: A few playing cards; a piece of thin transparent plastic or celluloid cut to the size of a playing card. A thick handkerchief, and a tall, wide glass.

• WHAT TO DO: Beforehand, place the plastic card beneath the group of playing cards. Spread the cards to show that there are several in the group, then throw the handkerchief over them. Push the plastic card into the centre of the cloth and ask someone to draw the card away in the handkerchief. Someone does, thinking that it is an actual playing card.

Lay the rest of the cards aside, take the plastic card through the cloth and push it down into the glass, or let someone else do so. Hold the glass high beneath the handkerchief, which you then pull away and show the glass apparently empty.

• WHAT HAPPENS: Due to the curved sides of the glass, the edges of the transparent card are totally obscured when people look directly through the glass and card. Actually, the supposed playing card has become invisible, even though it has not really vanished. The glass can even be turned about, provided it is kept in motion until the broad side is again toward the viewers.

• REMARKS: The glass can be laid aside and the transparent card can be reclaimed later. Or the rest of the cards can be pushed into the glass to show there is no trick about it. In drawing them out again, the plastic card is brought with them.

Making Money Multiply

• EFFECT: A sixpence is dropped into a clear, straight-walled drinking glass which is partly filled with water. A plate is set over the top of the glass so that nothing can leave or enter it. Glass and plate are then turned over together, with a most amazing result. The coin, falling to the plate, becomes a shilling, but the sixpence also remains within the glass, for it can be seen actually floating in the water just above the larger coin.

• MATERIALS: A sixpence, a glass containing water and a plate.

• WHAT TO DO: Drop the sixpence in the glass of water. Put the plate on top, take the glass in your right palm and press the plate downward with your left hand. A quick, bold turnover and the plate will be resting on your left palm, with the coin lying beneath the glass and the water still in the glass, but now contacting the plate. Let people look through the side of the glass at a downward angle and they will think they see a shilling on the plate and a sixpence above it.

Sixpence

Sixpence & Ghost Shilling

• WHAT HAPPENS: By viewing the surface of the water at just the right slant, you gain a view of the coin through the glass and directly into the water, producing a magnified image of the coin, like objects at the bottom of a goldfish bowl. But you also view the coin through the air within the glass and down through the surface of the water, which refracts the light rays and produces an image of a normal-sized coin near the surface, as in "An Appearing Coin," (p. 46.)

Easy Money

• EFFECT: Two shillings are shown on the palm of the outstretched left hand, one being in the open, the other covered by an inverted drinking glass. The glass is lifted and the coins are shaken in the fist, then dropped on the table. Instead of being worth only two shillings, their value has jumped to three shillings, for the coins are now a shilling and a florin.

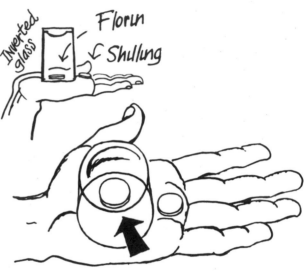

Inverted glass

Florin

Shilling

• MATERIALS: A shilling, a florin and a glass with a slightly curved bottom, as is common with most drinking glasses.

• WHAT TO DO: Lay the coins side by side, but invert the glass and cover the florin, before showing the coins in the palm of your hand. Viewed downward through the bottom of the glass, the florin will appear to be the same size as the shilling, making a total of two shillings. By simply laying the glass aside and shaking the coins, you can increase your money by half by showing that you hold a shilling and a florin.

• WHAT HAPPENS: The bottom of the glass acts as a reducing lens, which is just the opposite of a magnifying glass. Being side by side, the coins are easily compared and with a proper type of glass, the florin will appear as a shilling.

• REMARKS: With some glasses, the reduction is better when the glass is set right side up, with the florin just beneath the bottom. By testing various glasses, you can find the best type to use, whether inverted or kept with bottom down.

The Floating Ball

• EFFECT: A thimble is placed on each forefinger and when they are pointed together, a tiny metal ball floats between them.

• MATERIALS: Two metal thimbles.

• WHAT TO DO: Hold the fingers as with the "Surprise Sausage," then draw them slowly apart, until the image of a metal ball appears in the space between them, as you stare beyond.

• WHAT HAPPENS: The overlapping images

of the fingertips are confined to the thimbles as the fingers are separated. By adjusting the space and moving the hands closer or farther away, the thimbles produce the optical illusion of a suspended or magnetized ball.

Surprise Sausage

• EFFECT: The tips of the forefingers are held together directly in front of the eyes and a tiny sausage appears between them.

• MATERIALS: No special materials required.

• WHAT TO DO: Hold the tips of the forefingers together at a little less than arm's length and stare beyond them. Move the hands closer, if need be, until the sausage appears clearly.

• WHAT HAPPENS: Obstructing the distant view with the close-up of the fingers, causes the tips to form separate images, which blend into the optical illusion of a sausage.

Which Is Larger?

• EFFECT: Two curved pieces of cardboard, one red, the other blue, are placed upon the table. Someone is asked which is larger and he replies, "The blue," which happens to be below the red. But when the curved cards are transposed, with the blue above the red, everyone will be amazed to see that the red has become larger than the blue.

• MATERIALS: Two cardboard cut-outs, one

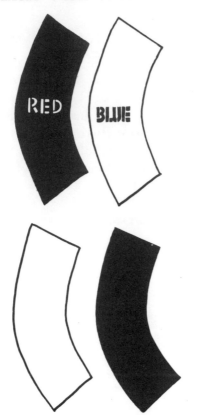

with his right eye. A hole appears in the palm of his hand and he sees straight through it.

• **MATERIALS:** A sheet of paper about 11 inches long.

• **WHAT TO DO:** Roll the paper into a tube one inch in diameter. Hold the tube to your right eye and place the side of your left hand against the middle of the tube, with your left palm directly toward your left eye. Keep both eyes open as you look through the tube and you will "see through" your left hand.

• **WHAT HAPPENS:** Since one eye is looking through the tube and other is looking at the hand, the two views blend to form an optical illusion of a hole in the centre of the left palm. A slight shifting of the tube may improve the illusion.

red, the other blue, which may be made to the exact size shown here.

• **WHAT TO DO:** Set the red cut-out above the blue, as shown in the first illustration. The blue will look larger than the red. Transpose them, as shown in the second illustration, and the red will appear larger than the blue.

• **WHAT HAPPENS:** Due to the curve of the cut-outs, they produce an optical illusion when one is placed above the other. Always, the lower cut-out will look larger. So by switching their positions, first the blue, then the red, will be classed as larger.

Crisscross Screen

• **EFFECT:** Within a square frame of light cardboard is a thin paper screen crisscrossed with horizontal, vertical, and diagonal lines. When the screen is placed upon a printed page, nothing can be read through it. Yet with a few "magic" words and a little action properly applied, the screen becomes transparent and the printing is revealed and read.

• **MATERIALS:** A sheet of tracing paper, meas-

X-Ray Tube

• **EFFECT:** A person holds his left hand alongside a paper tube and looks through the tube

uring 5 x 5 inches. A strip of cardboard, one inch wide, which can be cut into lengths and pasted around the edges as a frame, reducing the centre to 3 x 3 inches. The centre is further prepared by drawing lines on it with

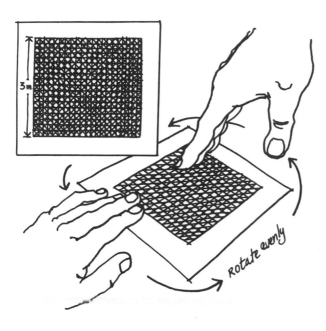

pencil and ruler, forming horizontal, vertical, and two diagonal rows, the lines being about an eighth of an inch apart, though this may be varied.

• **WHAT TO DO:** Set the crisscrossed screen over some printing or place it upon a specially lettered statement, as:

> YOU CAN READ
> THESE WORDS
> QUITE EASILY
> BY ROTATING
> THIS SCREEN
> WITH STEADY
> EASY ACTION

The lines on the tracing paper will render the words illegible. But by simply rotating the screen, running it over the letters in a circular fashion, the printing will spring to life and show right through the moving screen.

• **WHAT HAPPENS:** The constant motion allows a continuous view through the screen, like looking through the pickets of a fence or the uprights of a bridge railing, while riding past in a car. The cross-lines create a hazy effect, but they no longer completely obscure any part of the printed words as they did when the screen was motionless. This is a type of optical illusion that was used in early efforts to create motion pictures.

Restored Paper Napkin

• **EFFECT:** A paper napkin is torn in pieces which are rolled together and placed in a drinking glass. From a bottle, the demonstrator pours "invisible glue" into the glass. The torn napkin is brought from the glass and found to be completely restored.

• **MATERIALS:** Two identical paper napkins. A glass with ribbed or ornamental sides, but otherwise transparent. A piece of cardboard cut to fit vertically in the centre of the glass. A small sheet of aluminium, polished on both sides, which can be cut to the exact shape of the cardboard. An empty bottle.

• **WHAT TO DO:** Cut the aluminium to fit the glass and place it crosswise, separating the glass into two sections, front and back. When viewed directly from the front, the aluminium "fake"—as it is styled—acts as a mirror, so that the glass appears to be empty. Roll one napkin into a loose ball and thrust it down behind the mirror, where it remains perfectly concealed. Set the glass on the table. All this is done beforehand.

In your presentation, start by showing a paper napkin and openly tearing it into several pieces. Roll those into a ball and pick up the empty bottle, stating that it contains a magical "invisible glue." Rather than spill any of the priceless elixir, you decide to put the torn papers in a glass. So you lay aside the bottle and take the "mirror glass," showing it as though it were quite ordinary and empty. Push the torn papers down in front of the mirror, then turn to the table and as you do, give the glass a half turn so that the rear section is toward the audience. Set the glass on the table, pretend to pour liquid into the glass from the bottle, lay the bottle aside and draw the good napkin from the glass. Open the napkin and show it "restored."

• WHAT HAPPENS: By reflecting the front half of the glass, the mirror makes it look completely circular and therefore apparently a simple, empty glass; but the direct reflection also makes the mirror noticeable, particularly if it catches the light. That is where the ribbed glass plays a vital part. It diffuses the light rays so the reflection is somewhat indirect, yet still gives the glass a normal, circular effect.

Once the paper is in the glass, it hides the mirror sufficiently so that the glass can be turned around. The paper in the rear section looks like part of the original napkin that was inserted in front. The motion of the glass prevents the edge of the mirror being noticed during the turn.

The reflective quality of the aluminium does not need to be very high. Testing in the light will enable you to compare the appearance of the glass with and without the mirror in place, so you can see just how it should be held to appear empty. All in all, it makes a most interesting experiment in optics, even though the onlookers do not realize it.

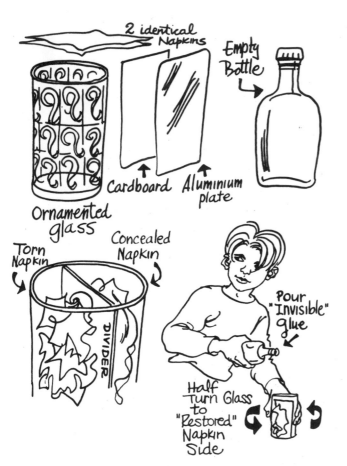

2 identical Napkins

Empty Bottle

Cardboard   Aluminium plate

Ornamented glass

Torn Napkin   Concealed Napkin

DIVIDER

Pour "Invisible" glue

Half Turn Glass to "Restored" Napkin Side

Shadow Monster

• EFFECT: When a person approaches the corner of a lighted room, the shadow of his head and shoulders naturally looms up ahead of him, completely black. But in this case, your shadow becomes very real, leering at you with bulging eyes and grinning mouth. It's enough to scare people, including yourself, if you didn't know the secret.

• MATERIALS: A fair-sized wall mirror. A sheet of paper about the size of the mirror. Some adhesive tape. An electric light.

• WHAT TO DO: Place the mirror on the side wall near the corner, so that the light, shining from a greater distance away, is reflected

• **REMARKS:** Proper placement of mirror and light are essential to this illusion. Whether to use a ceiling light or a floor lamp will depend upon the arrangement of the room. After experimenting beforehand, take your position, then have someone turn on the light, and the sudden appearance of the "shadow monster" will be startling and effective.

Candy from Nowhere

• **EFFECT:** A drinking glass is shown empty and is covered with a handkerchief. When the handkerchief is whisked away, the glass is filled with little candies, materialized from nowhere!

• **MATERIALS:** A glass, a shiny aluminium divider, some small hard candies, and a handkerchief.

• **WHAT TO DO:** Put the aluminium "fake" or divider in the glass, so it forms a "mirror glass" (as described with the "Restored Paper Napkin" on page 39). Fill the rear space

by the mirror, forming a lighted block on the end wall. Cut holes in the paper to represent eyes, nose and mouth; tape this to the mirror. Move your head and shoulders close to the end wall so your shadow appears there and it will take on the weird features of the mirror monster.

• **WHAT HAPPENS:** Once the paper is in place, it eliminates all the reflection except the cut-out features of the monster mask. Those still show in luminous form against the end wall. By bringing your head and shoulders still closer to the end wall, the reflected cut-outs show against your own shadow, since the reflection comes in at an angle from the more distant light.

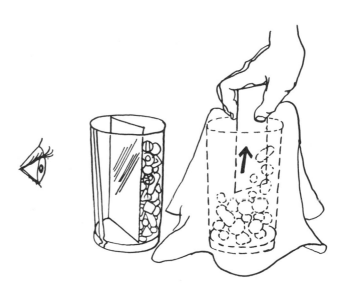

with the candy which remains hidden behind the fake.

In performing, show the glass apparently empty by keeping the mirror toward the onlookers. Cover the glass with the handkerchief and grip the fake through the cloth. Whisk the handkerchief away and pocket it, fake and all. The candy remains in the glass and can be poured on a plate, so the glass itself is quite ordinary at the finish.

• **WHAT HAPPENS:** The shiny aluminium fake gives the glass the appearance of being entirely empty. Only one side needs to be polished as the "mirror" effect is needed only in front, due to the removal of the divider. Small peanuts, or flaky cereal can be used instead of candy.

Through the Glass

• **EFFECT:** Two candlesticks with candles are set on opposite sides of a sheet of glass. When one candle is lighted, the other automatically appears to become lighted too.

• **MATERIALS:** Two candlesticks, two candles, a small sheet of window glass, two large books to prop the glass, and some matches.

• **WHAT TO DO:** Set the glass upright between the books. Place each candlestick with its candle an equal distance from the glass. Have people look straight at the candle on the near side, so they can see through the glass and observe the candle on the far side. Light the candle on the near side and they will see the flame ignite the far candle, with both flames continuing to burn.

• **WHAT HAPPENS:** When the lighted match is applied to the near candle, it throws its light against the glass, causing the flame to

be reflected as in a mirror. The far candle can still be seen through the glass, due to transparency, but its wick will appear to be lighted, due to the reflection producing an imaginary flame the same distance from the glass.

• **REMARKS:** Tests should be made beforehand to make sure the candles are placed at exact distances. A special frame can be made to support the glass if so desired. Also check the lighting of the room to make sure it is well suited for the illusion.

Magic Lamps

• **EFFECT:** A sheet of glass is set upright between two table lamps. When one lamp is turned on, the other becomes illuminated of its own accord.

• **MATERIALS:** Two identical table lamps, a sheet of glass, and two books or a frame to serve as a prop.

• **WHAT TO DO:** Set the glass exactly between the two lamps. Let people look from one side, so they see through to the other

lamp. Turn on the lamp on their side and both will light up.
• **WHAT HAPPENS:** This is simply a modernization of the two-candle experiment known

glass

Identical Lamps

Books for Support

as "Through the Glass." People see the reflected light from the near lamp and it gives the impression that the far lamp is also illuminated. However, since the electric light is much stronger than the candle flame, the entire lamp can be reflected, hence it must be perfectly placed to blend with the far lamp.
• **REMARKS:** If the light in the room is very subdued to start, the far lamp will be scarcely visible when the near lamp is turned on. In that case, the reflection of the near lamp will be accepted in its entirety as representing the far lamp. Still, the images should be synchronized as well as possible, otherwise the far lamp will produce a "ghost" effect of the type sometimes encountered during a television show.

Rub Away Coin

• **EFFECT:** Three large coins are held with thumbs and fingers at each side. The coins

are rubbed back and forth, but when the action ceases, one coin has been rubbed away, leaving only two.
• **MATERIALS:** Two large coins.

• **WHAT TO DO:** Hold the two coins so they overlap and keep thrusting them back and forth with thumbs above and fingers below. Tell people to "Watch the three coins" and then add, "Now one has been rubbed away." Drop the two coins on the table and they will be quite amazed, for until then, they will be sure they saw three coins.
• **WHAT HAPPENS:** In rubbing the coins as described, the lower coin appears elongated as it emerges in front and back of the upper coin. This creates an optical illusion of three coins instead of only two. A steady, rhythmic motion is more effective than too much speed.

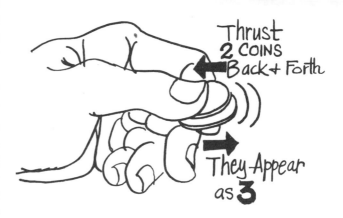

Thrust 2 COINS Back + Forth

They Appear as **3**

Coin Gone

• **EFFECT:** A coin is placed on the palm of the left hand and a glass of water is set on the coin. Looking down through the water, observers see the coin. Then, suddenly, you make it vanish.

• **MATERIALS:** A glass almost filled with water. A coin.

• **WHAT TO DO:** Set the coin and glass on your left hand and let everyone view the coin as described. Press your right palm squarely on top of the glass. When they look for the coin it will be gone.

• **WHAT HAPPENS:** Your right hand cuts off a direct look down through the water. People must now look through the side of the glass, from an angle beginning beneath the surface of the water. Due to the refraction of the light rays, they can't quite see to the bottom of the glass, so the coin is rendered invisible.

Coin and Glass

• **EFFECT:** A transparent drinking glass is standing upside down on a dinner table with a coin lying beside it. A paper napkin is wrapped around the glass, which is then placed over the coin. When the napkin is removed, the coin has vanished. Everyone can look down through the glass and see that the coin is not there. But when the glass is again covered by the napkin and lifted away, the coin returns.

• **MATERIALS:** A table with a white or plain-coloured cloth. A drinking glass. A paper disk of the same diameter as the mouth of the glass and the same colour as the tablecloth. A paper napkin.

• **WHAT TO DO:** Beforehand, paste the paper disk to the mouth of the glass, making sure it fits exactly, even if the edges must be

slightly trimmed. Invert the glass on the table, lay the coin beside it and you are ready to perform.

Wrap the paper napkin around the glass, making sure that it is completely covered, so that the paper disk will not be seen when you lift the glass. As soon as you place the glass over the coin, it is safe to remove the napkin, as the paper disk looks like part of the tablecloth. The coin, being beneath the paper, has vanished. To bring it back, you simply reverse the process.

• **WHAT HAPPENS:** Actually, this is an optical illusion in which the paper is mistaken for the tablecloth, both being the same in colour. The curve of the glass helps the illusion and the rim hides the edge of the paper disk, so that the disappearance and return of the coin is automatic.

Coin, Ring, and Card

• **EFFECT:** A thick ring, two inches or more in diameter, is resting on a sheet of brightly coloured paper, with a square of plain cardboard beside it. A penny is set on the paper and the ring is placed around it with the cardboard on top. When the card is lifted, the coin has vanished, only to return in the same mysterious manner.

• **MATERIALS:** A large key ring, curtain ring, or any ring of a similar type. A paper disk, the same diameter as the ring, and matching the colour of the paper sheet, which should be at least 6 or 8 inches square. A cardboard square slightly larger than the ring. A penny.

• **WHAT TO DO:** Paste the paper disk to the bottom of the ring. When the ring is laid on the sheet of paper, people think they see clear through the ring, since the disk matches the sheet. Lay the coin beside the ring, cover the ring with the card, and place both over the coin. Lift the card and the coin has apparently vanished from within the ring. A reversal of the action will bring it back.

But that is only part. By way of variation, you can drop the coin into the ring as it lies on the table; then cover the ring with the card. Ring and card are lifted together and laid aside. The coin has apparently vanished, having been carried away by the paper disk. Put the ring back where it was, with the card still on top. Lift the card and the coin will reappear within the ring.

• **WHAT HAPPENS:** This works on the same principle as the "Coin and Glass," the paper disk matching the sheet and thereby hiding the coin. The disk is also unsuspected when used to take away the coin. A brightly coloured paper, or a sheet with a mottled design will make the optical illusion more effective.

An Appearing Coin

- **EFFECT:** A large coin is placed in the very centre of a fair-sized bowl, which is set on a table some distance from an observer, who is seated in a chair. Because of the angle, the person cannot quite see the coin. Yet without touching or moving either the coin or the bowl, the coin is made to appear before the observer's fixed gaze.
- **MATERIALS:** A coin, a bowl, a pitcher of water. A table and a chair.
- **WHAT TO DO:** Seat the person so that the

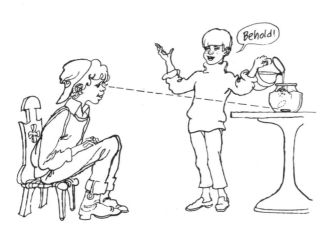

coin is just below his angle of vision. While he watches, pour water from the pitcher into the bowl, carefully and slowly, so as not to disturb the coin. By the time you have nearly filled the bowl, the coin will have appeared for the observer.

- **WHAT HAPPENS:** Due to the refraction of the water, the light rays are bent at an angle, bringing more of the bottom of the bowl into view. During the pouring of the water, the bottom of the bowl will actually seem to rise, but so imperceptibly that the observer will not know it until the coin comes into his bent line of vision; and even then, he may not know why.

Metal Through Metal

- **EFFECT:** Two large safety pins are linked together and then clamped. A quick, simple pull, and the pins come apart, yet remain as solidly clamped as before.
- **MATERIALS:** Two large safety pins.
- **WHAT TO DO:** Close one pin, "A," with its loose bar to the left and its head extending outward as you hold the small end between your left thumb and forefinger. With the right hand, hold the second pin, "B," by the small end, between thumb and forefinger with the loose bar to the left and the head pointing outward.

The larger the pins, the better, as they allow a firmer grip at the lower end. If you find that the pins tend to slip, use a larger size.

Slide the head of pin "B" downward between the bars of pin "A," so the head goes under the loose bar of "A." The loose bar of "B" goes over or above the loose bar of "A." Pin "B" is then clamped shut and the hands resume their holds on the small ends of their respective pins. "A" being held by the left hand; "B" by the right.

All is then ready for the vital action. Draw the pins apart by bringing them head to head, tilting both heads inward and giving

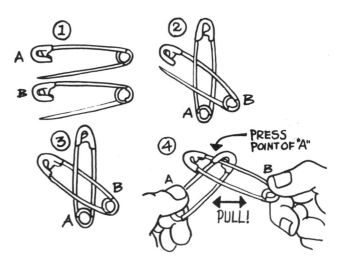

a quick, smooth pull. A neat, sliding motion will separate them without unlocking them.

• **What Happens:** Actually, the solid bar of the right hand pin, "B," does unlock the loose bar of the left-hand pin, "A." But with the bars almost parallel, the opening is so slight that pin "B" comes free before the loose bar of pin "A" is fully unclamped. As a result, pin "A" relocks itself, as it is designed to do, whenever its loose bar engages the specially constructed head. That is what makes a safety pin safe and it also makes this experiment a good one.

Mirror Image

• **Effect:** Some long words and a long row of figures are written on a pad, which is then held in front of a mirror. A person is asked to read off the words and the numbers, which he does slowly and with difficulty because the letters and figures are reversed in the mirrored image. Yet *you* can look into the mirror and read them off without the slightest pause!

• **Materials:** Two mirrors, preferably a wall mirror and a hand mirror. A pad and pencil.

• **What To Do:** Print some words like IN-COMPREHENSIBLE or ANTEDILUVIAN on the pad, along with a row of figures, as 3515429076384. Have someone hold the writing toward the hand mirror and try to read it in reverse. Let someone else do the same with the wall mirror. When your turn comes, hold the writing toward the wall mirror with your left hand, then turn away and pick up the hand mirror with your right hand. Hold the hand mirror so you can look back over your left shoulder and see the reflection of the pad in the wall mirror. Reading the

words and the numbers then becomes simplicity itself.

• **What Happens:** By using both mirrors as described, the writing reversed in one is again reversed in the other, which brings it back to normal, so it can be read off rapidly. It is a case of doubling up a scientific principle to neutralize the effect.

• **Remarks:** Let anyone write words and numbers for you to read in a mirror, but specify that the letters and figures be printed large. Another mode of operation is to hold the writing and the hand mirror both toward the wall mirror, but turn the pad 45° to the right and the hand mirror 45° to the left. Then look toward the right and read the message in the hand mirror.

The Roaming Coin

• **Effect:** A coin is dropped within a large ring, which is covered with a card and moved away, leaving the coin in full view. The coin is covered with another ring and card. Both cards are lifted and the coin amazingly has roamed from one ring to the other.

• **MATERIALS:** Identical with those used in the "Coin, Ring, and Card," but in this case, a second ring is used. It is prepared with a paper disk exactly like the first ring, and also has a square card to go with it. A duplicate coin is also required.

• **WHAT TO DO:** Have the two rings lying on the sheet of matching paper. Have the duplicate coin under Ring "A," at the left. Both rings are uncovered, but appear empty. Lay the coin within "A," cover the ring with its card and lift both together, placing them beyond Ring "B," which is near the centre.

People see the duplicate coin at the spot where you picked up "A" and suppose it to be the original coin, which normally would have stayed there. Now, cover "B" with its card and place it over the visible coin at the left. Lift the cards from both rings. The coin will be gone from Ring "B" at the left and will be seen reposing in Ring "A" at the right, which is baffling indeed.

• **WHAT HAPPENS:** The two principles used in "Coin, Ring, and Card" are simply worked in combination. The first coin is taken away by the disk pasted to Ring "A"; the disk pasted to Ring "B" covers the duplicate coin and conceals it. You can repeat the experiment by taking the coin from within the ring at the right and dropping it in the ring at the left, then going through original routine. At the finish, cover each ring with its card and drop them in your pockets, with the extra coin.

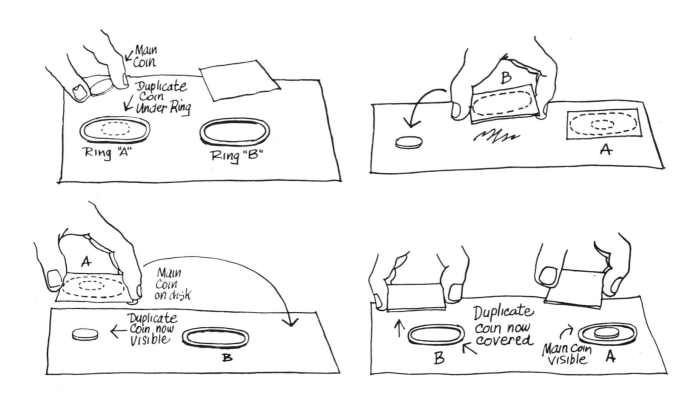

Maginertia

Tricks Involving Inertia

Nine Coins

- **EFFECT:** Nine coins are placed in a row in groups of threes, with a space of an inch or more between each group. All in one quick action, a coin is moved from the group at the right to the centre group, while another coin is moved from the centre to the left. Yet this is done without touching either of the moved coins in any way whatever, while none of the other coins is moved more than a trifling fraction of an inch.

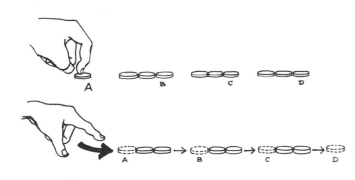

- **MATERIALS:** Ten coins, all of the same size. A smooth surface, like a polished wooden table top.

- **WHAT TO DO:** Line up nine coins in groups of three, with spaces between. All must be in an exact row, the spaces to be determined by experiment. After stating your purpose, as already described, bring out the tenth coin and lay it a few inches to the right of the broken row. With your finger, give it a hard slide against the first coin in the group on the right. A coin will slide from that group and join the centre group. That coin, in turn, will send the far coin of the centre group to the group on the left.

- **WHAT HAPPENS:** Inertia causes the intervening coins to remain practically unmoved, but the force of the arriving coin is transferred to the free coin at the other end of the group. That coin is sent to the centre group, where the same thing happens again, sending another free coin on its way, but with diminished effect, so that the group at the left remains undisturbed as it receives the coin.

A Remarkable Nutcracker

- **EFFECT:** A table knife is suspended by a thread from the top of a doorway. A walnut is placed directly below the knife and the thread is clipped with scissors. The knife drops down and cracks the walnut.
- **MATERIALS:** A nail or push-pin, a thread, a knife, some adhesive tape, a walnut, and a glass of water. Scissors.
- **WHAT TO DO:** Fix the nail in the top of the doorway and tie one end of the thread around it. Tape the other end of the thread near the tip of the knife blade, so the handle points straight downward, five or six feet

above the floor. Lay the walnut on the floor beneath the knife. All is then ready for the test.

Bring the glass of water straight up toward the knife so that the handle of the knife is partly immersed, but the knife still hangs free. Lower the glass, put it aside and watch the drop of water that falls from the knife handle. Move the walnut to the spot where the drop strikes and watch succeeding drops until they actually land squarely on the walnut.

The experiment is then in order. Cut the thread with a quick snip. The knife will drive straight down and the handle will hit the walnut full force, cracking it wide open.

• **WHAT HAPPENS:** The law of gravity causes all objects to fall directly toward the centre of the earth. Each drop of water therefore marks the path that the knife will follow, provided it is hung straight downward. The heavy handle gives the knife a low centre of gravity, which also contributes to its exact fall.

• **REMARKS:** This experiment requires considerable preparation, but it is worth it, and therefore should be given due care. Make sure the knife is heavy enough and that it is properly suspended, either by taping the thread straight down the blade or tying it around the blade. Keep the knife steady and immerse the handle repeatedly if further study of the water drops proves necessary.

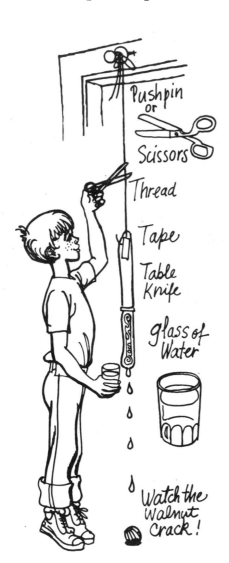

Pushpin or
Scissors
Thread
Tape
Table Knife
Glass of Water
Watch the Walnut Crack!

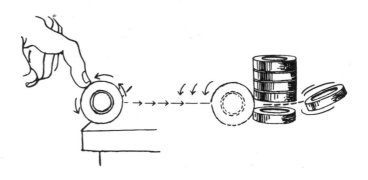

Stacked Checkers

• **EFFECT:** Six checkers are stacked, all blacks, except for a red checker next to the bottom black. Another red checker is set on its edge and snapped along the table. It hits the stack and knocks out the lone red checker, leaving the blacks intact.

• **MATERIALS:** Two red checkers and five black checkers. A flat table surface.

• **WHAT TO DO:** Stack the checkers with a red second from the bottom. Stand the other red on edge and aim it at the stack, pressing your forefinger firmly on the top of the checker. Then give the finger a hard, downward snap on the near edge. This spins the checker toward you, but at the same time shoots it along the table so it hits the stack. Done correctly, it will knock the other red checker cleanly from the stack.

• **WHAT HAPPENS:** The side of the snapped checker hits at the exact level of the stacked red checker, knocking it forward. If the snapped checker continued forward, it would wreck the stack as well; but due to the reverse spin, it recoils instantly, taking no effect whatever on the black checkers. That brings another scientific principle into play; inertia. So suddenly is the red checker punched from the stack that the blacks above it simply drop of their own weight, and the stack stays intact.

part a spinning action, but is easier. Give the raw eggs to your friends and watch them try to do the trick without results.

• **WHAT HAPPENS:** A hard-boiled egg, having a fixed balance point, is similar to a toy top and therefore will spin like one. The inertia of the fluid contents of a raw egg prevents it from doing the same.

• **REMARKS:** This is a very handy experiment when starting on a picnic. You can make sure that you are taking along hard-boiled eggs by spinning them before packing them in the basket.

The Dropping Eggs

• **EFFECT:** The scientific magician displays a setup of equipment worthy of a stage performance. Four tall glasses filled with water are standing on a solid table. Mounted on

The Spinning Egg

• **EFFECT:** An egg is snapped between the thumb and fingers, so that it spins like a top. It seems very easy until other people try it only to find that their eggs just won't spin.

• **MATERIALS:** Several eggs, all raw except one, which is hard-boiled. A plate on which to spin the egg.

• **WHAT TO DO:** Snap the hard-boiled egg as described, or hold it upright between the palms and thrust one hand forward while drawing the other back, which will also im-

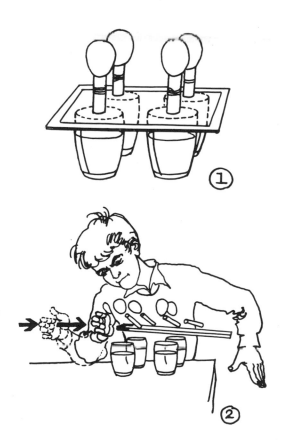

the glasses is a tray, and upon it are four large spools of thread, each directly above a glass. Surmounting the spools are four eggs, each balanced on its large end. A tricky arrangement indeed, but what follows is even trickier. With a hard, quick stroke, the tray and spools are knocked away and the eggs drop squarely into the glasses, splashing the water high as they land there unbroken.

• **MATERIALS:** Four tall glasses filled with water, a light, thin tray, four spools and four eggs. Instead of the tray, a square of board or stiff plastic may be used, while four old playing cards, each rolled into a tube and girded with a rubber band, can be used as substitutes for the spools. As a special precaution, the eggs should be hard-boiled, particularly when trying out the experiment.

• **WHAT TO DO:** Set up the apparatus as al-

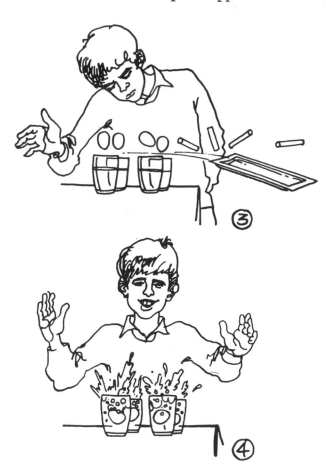

ready described, letting the onlookers watch you put everything in place, unless you are already fixed. Setting it up openly is preferable, however, as it proves there is no deception. When all is ready, hold your hand level with one end of the tray and deliver a hard, quick stroke, stopping immediately after hitting the tray. In fact, the hand should then be whipped back rather than risk any "follow through." The tray scales away, the spools scatter, but the eggs plop serenely in the glasses in a manner truly magical.

• **WHAT HAPPENS:** Inertia is responsible for the behaviour of the four eggs. Stationary objects tend to remain so, unless some force or action puts them into motion. If the tray had been pushed slowly from the glasses, the spools and eggs would simply have toppled along with it. But by hitting it hard, the tray and spools are knocked away so rapidly that very little lateral force is applied to the eggs; hence inertia lets them drop downward.

Note that other scientific factors are at work here. There is friction between the tray and the glass rims. If the glasses were empty and a heavy tray were used, enough force would be applied to the glasses to topple them. But the weight of the water stabilizes the glasses and the use of a light tray lessens the friction, so the glasses stay where they are.

The weight of the eggs presses the light spools firmly against the tray and there, friction takes over. The tray carries the spools along with it, but the contact between spools and eggs is so quickly eliminated that the effect on the eggs is scarcely appreciable and does not disturb their vertical fall.

• **REMARKS:** The illustrations showing the stages of this unusual experiment were made directly from a series of high-speed camera pictures that caught the action in hundredths of a second. Note how the spools are carried away immediately (Fig. 2) and how they scatter when the tray is fully clear (Fig. 3).

Such high-speed photos were needed to reveal the effect upon the eggs, which are turning in the direction of the stroke (Fig. 2) so that they land almost sidewise in the glasses (Fig. 4) which should therefore be sufficiently wide-mouthed to receive the eggs comfortably.

usually make that mistake, so you can still baffle them when you do the trick again.

• REMARKS: By folding a paper into a double or triple pleat, it will be strong enough to support a coin. Use staples or paste to form the ends into a permanent loop. Practice the stroke until you can do it deftly, and few if any observers will note that you are hooking the loop instead of hitting it.

One Quick Stroke

• EFFECT: A band of fairly stiff paper is set upright on a glass, and a coin is placed on top of the loop. The paper is knocked away with a pencil and the coin falls into the glass.

• MATERIALS: A loop of paper about one inch wide, which can be three inches or more in diameter. A small glass with a narrow mouth. A long pencil.

• WHAT TO DO: Set loop on glass, put a coin on top, and make a long, hard sweep with the end of the pencil, going past the outer portion of the loop and hooking it from the inside, so that the pencil carries the loop away and the coin drops in the glass.

• WHAT HAPPENS: The sudden removal of the loop leaves the coin unsupported, and due to its inertia, the coin drops squarely into the glass. However, this would not happen if you hit the loop from the outside, as you would then knock away the loop and coin together. When other people try it, they

The Balanced Coin

• EFFECT: A narrow strip of paper is placed over the edge of a drinking glass and a coin is balanced flat upon it. Without touching either the glass or the coin, you remove the

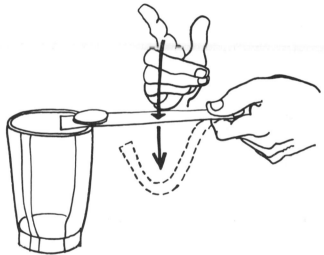

paper, leaving the coin still balanced on the glass rim.

• MATERIALS: A coin, a drinking glass, and a strip of paper about 6 inches long and ¾-inch wide.

• WHAT TO DO: First, test the coin to see that it balances nicely on the rim. Then lay one end of the paper over the edge so that about an inch projects inward, and balance

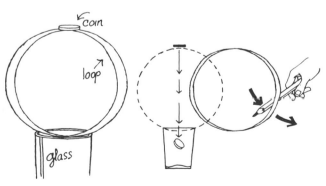

the coin carefully on the strip. Lift the other end of the strip with your left hand and hold it horizontally while you give the centre of the strip a sharp downstroke with your right forefinger. This will whisk away the paper, leaving the coin balanced on the glass.

• **WHAT HAPPENS:** Inertia is responsible, the weight of the coin holding it steadily in place while the light paper is so suddenly removed. The friction from the glass edge is so slight that the coin remains undisturbed.

• **REMARKS:** If the coin won't balance at the start, use another glass. Also, make sure it is properly balanced after the paper is in place. Compare this with the "Balanced Bottles" (Page 54).

Balanced Bottles

• **EFFECT:** A bank-note is placed on the rim of a soda bottle, and another bottle of the same size is set upside down on top, so that one bottle is balanced precariously on the

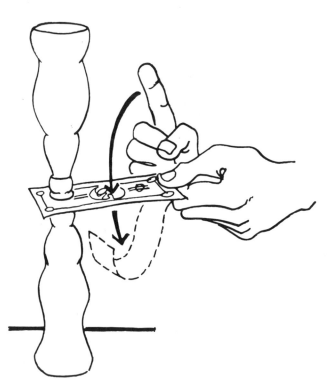

other, with the bank-note between. With a quick, deft move, you take away the bank-note, leaving the bottles still balanced.

• **MATERIALS:** Two empty soda bottles. A bank-note. Play money, or a sheet of paper cut to size can be used instead of the note.

• **WHAT TO DO:** Balance the bottles very carefully by holding the bank-note with your other hand, keeping the note toward one end, rather than centring it between the bottle rims. Draw the note taut with one hand, then extend the forefinger of the other hand and hit the bank-note near the centre, with a quick hard downstroke. The note will whip away, leaving the bottles balanced.

• **WHAT HAPPENS:** Here we see a very fine example of inertia. The slightest impulse given to the upper bottle would cause it to topple and fall, but due to its weight, the removal of the paper is trifling and therefore has no perceptible effect upon the balanced bottle.

• **REMARKS:** Be sure to have the bottles balanced exactly at the start, rather than let the paper help in balancing them. Keep the note stretched straight out, horizontally, when you strike it. If you wish, you can present this as a puzzle, stating that you will remove the note without touching either bottle.

Flip It!

• **EFFECT:** A playing card is set over the mouth of a small glass and a coin is set on top. With one quick flip, the card is removed and the coin is dropped into the glass.

• **MATERIALS:** A glass, a playing card and a coin, preferably a fairly large one.

• **WHAT TO DO:** Set up the glass, card and coin as described. Bend the tip of a finger in against your thumb, then snap the finger outward against a corner of the card, which skims away, dropping the coin into the glass.

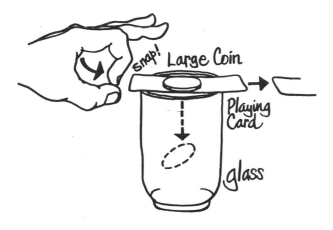

• **WHAT HAPPENS:** The quick flip literally shoots the card out from under the coin. The friction is so slight that the inertia of the heavy coin drops it straight down into the glass.

Turn It Over

• **EFFECT:** You lay a coin flat on your up-turned wrist. Without touching it in any other way, you make the coin turn over, so it lies tails instead of head, yet is still on your wrist.

• **MATERIALS:** A coin.

• **WHAT TO DO:** Place the coin flat on your wrist, quite close to the heel of your hand. Give your thumb and second finger a hard snap, repeating the action as often as necessary. The right snap will turn the coin over.

• **WHAT HAPPENS:** The force of the snap is transmitted to the wrist muscles, as you will observe when you try the experiment. It takes a hard snap and a certain knack, but the muscular action is sufficient to flip the coin completely over.

Equilitrix

*Feats of Equilibrium
and Balance*

The Balanced Pencil

• **EFFECT:** A brightly coloured pencil is set on end and remains balanced. It is handed to another person to try the experiment, but now it will not balance, for it needs the "magic" touch.

• **MATERIALS:** A pencil with an end of brass or other metal of slightly less diameter than the pencil proper. A piece of pliable plastic a little more than an inch in length and slightly wider than the metal cap of the pencil. Some transparent mending tape.

• **WHAT TO DO:** Roll the plastic around the cap of the pencil so it fits snugly; then roll enough tape around the plastic to hold it in place. This must be done carefully and exactly so that the edge of the tiny tube is perfectly even. This is the unsuspected "gimmick" on which the balance depends.

Start with the gimmick already on the end of the pencil. With a little practice, you can balance the pencil on that end. Later, pick up the pencil at that end, holding it lightly between your thumb and fingers. Extend the pencil to someone, telling him to try the balancing experiment. As he takes the pencil, you retain the gimmick. When he tries to balance the pencil by itself, he fails.

• **WHAT HAPPENS:** The edge of the gimmick being even, it forms a little base that keeps the pencil upright. Being transparent, the

tiny plastic cylinder cannot be seen, so the pencil appears to be balancing of its own accord. Without the gimmick, the pencil must actually be balanced on end, which is impossible as the metal cap is smooth and either slightly rounded or irregular, rendering it unstable.

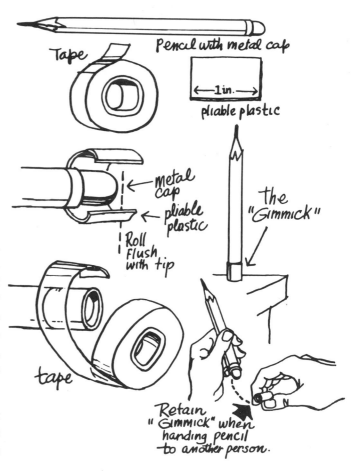

Tape

Pencil with metal cap

← 1 in. →

pliable plastic

metal cap

pliable plastic

Roll Flush with tip

the "Gimmick"

tape

Retain "Gimmick" when handing pencil to another person.

Another Balanced Pencil

• **EFFECT:** The point of a pencil is set on the tip of the finger in an effort to balance the pencil upright. Impossible though this seems, it is soon accomplished, and in an unexpected way.

• **MATERIALS:** A pencil and a penknife.

• **WHAT TO DO:** After showing how you intend to balance the pencil, bring out the penknife, open its blade, and press its point firmly into the pencil, at an upward angle just above the pencil point. Close the knife part way, so its bulk comes in at an angle below the pencil, which can then be balanced on your fingertip.

• **WHAT HAPPENS:** The knife acts as a counterweight, bringing the centre of gravity down from the upright pencil to the knife itself. The pencil becomes a sort of hook which is hung on the finger, making the balance very simple.

Amazing Paper Napkin

• **EFFECT:** A paper napkin is held at one corner by the right hand. The left hand raises the opposite corner and the napkin stays balanced in an upright position.

• **MATERIALS:** A paper napkin. A few extras if needed.

• **WHAT TO DO:** In taking the napkin by diagonal corners, pull it taut, carefully but steadily. Repeat this a few times, taking care not to tear the napkin. It can then be raised by one end and balanced by the other.

• **WHAT HAPPENS:** The pulling process stretches the fibres of the paper and lengthens the napkin along one diagonal, drawing the side corners inward. This gives the napkin a temporary rigidity which makes the balance possible.

• **REMARKS:** If torn, a napkin should be discarded and another used instead.

Bewildering Butterfly

• **EFFECT:** A lifelike imitation of a full-sized butterfly is placed on the tip of the forefinger or a pencil, its head making only the slightest contact. Yet the butterfly poises there, with no other support.

• MATERIALS: A piece of thin cardboard, cut to the shape of a large butterfly and appropriately decorated. Two small metal washers or small coins. A rounded toothpick or a large wooden match without a head. Some mending tape.

• WHAT TO DO: Affix the toothpick lengthwise beneath the butterfly so that one end becomes the head, extending slightly from between the wings, while the other end becomes the tail. Fasten the two weights at the very front corners of the wings, keeping them

beneath, so they are out of sight. Test this until the head becomes the perfect balance point; then:

Show the butterfly from above, holding the tail between thumb and fingers of one hand. Rest the head on your other forefinger and release the butterfly, leaving it balanced there. The same applies to the tip of a pencil, a knife blade or some similar object. .

• WHAT HAPPENS: By setting the weights forward, they counteract the weight of the wings and body, so that the head represents the centre of gravity and serves as a balance point.

• REMARKS: If the fronts of the wings are folded under and decorated beneath, both sides of the butterfly can be shown, as the

weights will be hidden. Care in construction of the butterfly will add to the effectiveness of this experiment.

Turnover Match Pack

• EFFECT: An empty match pack is bent slightly and set upright on the table. The moment the fingers release the pack, it does a complete somersault, landing with its curved side upward. This surprising action can be repeated, time after time.

• MATERIALS: An empty match pack.

• WHAT TO DO: Close an empty match pack and press the top and bottom toward each other to form an inward curve. Take the bottom of the pack between thumb and fingers and set it upside down on the table, keeping it nearly upright. As you release it, tip it just enough so that it falls on its outward curve and it will make a complete and surprising turnover.

• WHAT HAPPENS: The striking surface with its layers of cardboard makes the bottom of the match pack much heavier than the top, hence the centre of gravity is very high when the pack is inverted. When released, it would normally fall flat immediately, but the curved back turns this into a revolving motion. This gives it such momentum that the top of the pack continues on past the balance point and the pack lands front downward.

• REMARKS: The turnover will become more rapid if the curve .is increased, but it is very

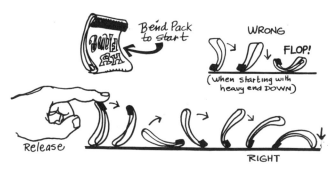

effective if kept to a lazy flip-flop. It then reminds you of a roller coaster gathering enough speed on a downward chute to carry it over the next hump, which makes the experiment all the more intriguing because of the scientific factors involved.

Top Side Up

• **EFFECT:** Another match pack is curved inward and held with its top side up. When released, it does a complete turnover.

• **MATERIALS:** An empty match pack, a weight like a small bolt or screw. Some mending tape.

• **WHAT TO DO:** Affix the bolt inside the match pack at the top, using the tape to hold it there. Close the pack and curve it inward by pressing top and bottom toward each other. When ready for the experiment, set the match pack upright on the bottom end, release it so it falls on its outward curve and it will turn a somersault.

• **WHAT HAPPENS:** Again, it is a case of having the heavy end upward, so that the high centre of gravity causes a rapid turnover,

with the momentum providing a follow-through, as with the ordinary "Turnover Match Pack." In this case, even keen observers are unaware that the top is the heavy end instead of the bottom, which adds a baffling angle to the scientific experiment.

• **REMARKS:** This is a good sequel to the "Turnover Match Pack." By having the weighted pack handy, it can be introduced before people catch on to the simpler experiment. They suddenly see you setting a match pack top side up, yet it works just the same. Be careful, of course, to use a short bolt that will not show at the sides of the closed pack.

Egg on End

• **EFFECT:** An egg is carefully set on a table and balanced on its large end. This duplicates the famous feat attributed to Columbus. When other people try it, the egg topples.

• **MATERIALS:** An egg. A pinch of salt.

• **WHAT TO DO:** Moisten the end of the egg and dip it in the salt so that some granules adhere to the egg. Set the egg carefully on a level table, with or without a cloth, and it will balance there.

• **WHAT HAPPENS:** An egg normally rests on its side, because then its centre of gravity is as low as possible. When set on end, it as-

sumes a state of unstable equilibrium, which can only be momentarily neutralized before the egg topples to its side, to resume its stable state. But it is possible to hold it in that temporary balance and the grains of salt provide just enough foundation for it.

• **REMARKS:** By secretly dipping the egg in the salt beforehand, you can mystify observers with this experiment, particularly if you demonstrate it on a table with a light-coloured surface or cloth. By brushing away the adhering grains in picking up the egg, it can be given to other persons who will try the trick and fail.

The Balanced Forks

• **EFFECT:** Two forks, extending in opposite directions, are balanced on the rim of a glass, along with a borrowed coin.

• **MATERIALS:** Two table forks, a drinking glass, and a coin chosen because of its size.

• **WHAT TO DO:** Point the prongs of the forks in an inward direction and thrust them together, so that the forks are interlocked. Press a coin between the upper prongs from the inner side. Rest the coin on the far side of the glass rim, so the handles of the fork extend in your direction. By properly adjust-

ing the forks, you can make the coin balance on its side, keeping the forks balanced with it.

• **WHAT HAPPENS:** The handles of the forks serve as a counterbalance for the coin and prongs. Precarious though it looks, it is like adjusting weights on an ordinary pair of scales, the only difference being the articles used.

• **REMARKS:** Choice of forks with pliable prongs is important; also glasses should be tested to find which has the most suitable rim. The coin is important, as it should fit between the prongs just snugly enough to stay there. With a good combination of such articles, the very edge of the coin can sometimes be balanced on the glass rim with the forks absolutely steady.

The Knife Stand

• **EFFECT:** Three table knives are neatly and cleverly arranged to form a solid metal stand that will support a heavy object.

• **MATERIALS:** Three table knives of the same size. A glass of water or some other suitable object.

• **WHAT TO DO:** Point the knives together

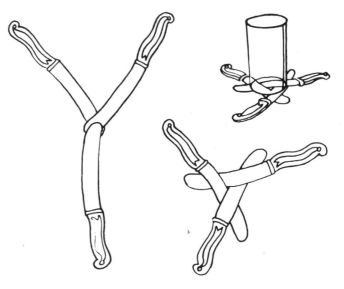

so they form a "Y." Slide the point of the lower knife over the blade from the left, close to the handle. Slide the blade from the right under the point of the knife from the left; then work the point from the right over the blade of the lower knife, close to the handle. Tighten the blades and they will form a criss-crossed tripod capable of supporting a heavy weight.

• WHAT HAPPENS: Due to the interlocking arrangement, each blade supports another, making this a simple but enlightening experiment in structural engineering. The tripod can be used as a coaster or trivet to keep hot objects from injuring a table surface.

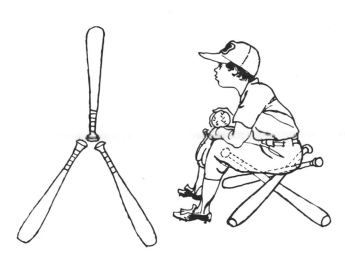

Three Baseball Bats

• EFFECT: Three baseball bats are arranged to form a firm stool capable of supporting a person's weight.

• MATERIALS: Three baseball bats of similar size.

• WHAT TO DO: Point the small ends of the bats together like a "Y" and slide them over and under one another exactly as with the "Knife Stand." The result will be a low but strong stool.

• WHAT HAPPENS: Each bat supports another on the same principle as the "Knife Stand."

• REMARKS: This device can be of practical use to players, saving them from sitting on the damp ground.

Lift Five with One

• EFFECT: Five drinking straws are laid on the table. They are so arranged that by lifting just one straw, the other four will come up with it, all being firmly in position.

• MATERIALS: Five drinking straws.

• WHAT TO DO: Lay two straws ("A" and "B") lengthwise, about three inches apart, and hump the centre of each straw upward. Lay two more straws ("C" and "D") so they form an "X," each straw crossing over straws "A" and "B." Hold all these firmly against the table with the palm and outspread fingers of the left hand.

With the right hand, flatten the end of another straw ("E") and slide it from right to left under the centre of "B," then up over the crossing of "C" and "D," then down under the centre of "A." This requires careful shifting of the fingers and if any straw goes awry, it should promptly be worked back into place.

When "E" emerges at the left side of the

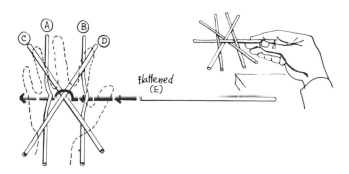

layout, lift it by the right end and all five straws will come up together.

• WHAT HAPPENS: The straws are interlaced so that they form supports for one another in a truly scientific fashion, turning a comparatively simple experiment into a study of basic structural requirements.

The Balanced Potato

• EFFECT: A potato is balanced end upward on the rim of a tall glass. It sounds impossible, but proves to be quite simple when you call in the aid of two handy table utensils.

• MATERIALS: A tall drinking glass, a small raw potato and two table forks of identical size.

• WHAT TO DO: Push the prongs of a fork upward in one side of the potato. Then do the same with the second fork on the other side, so the handles extend downward at about the same angle. Rest the lower end of the potato on your fingers to see if you can balance it; if not, change the position of whichever fork will help. Once it is satisfactory, place the lower end on the glass

rim and balance the potato there, with the forks hanging below.

• WHAT HAPPENS: The hanging handles of the forks serve as counterbalances, by bringing the centre of gravity far below the bottom of the potato. Thus, the potato, though too unstable to be balanced by itself, becomes a link between the prongs of the counterbalanced forks. As such it can be readily balanced.

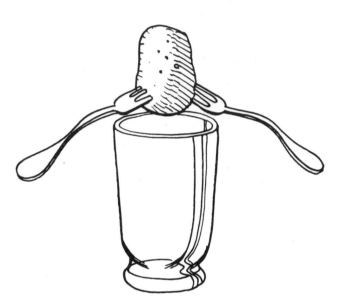

Hydromagic

Tricks with Water and Liquids

Amazing Grape Seed

• **Effect:** A grape seed is dropped into a glass of soda water. It sinks, then rises to the top, then sinks again, only to rise, practically at command. This continues indefinitely.

• **Materials:** A glass of plain soda and a grape seed.

• **What To Do:** Drop the grape seed in the soda water and sit back to watch what happens. At intervals, you can snap your fingers to make the seed sink or rise to the surface. But the snap is mere byplay. The grape seed really does the trick itself.

• **What Happens:** The seed sinks, because it is heavier than water, but not too much so. For as it lies at the bottom of the glass, bubbles from the soda water naturally attach themselves to the seed. When enough bubbles have gathered, they provide sufficient buoyancy to bring the seed to the surface. There, the bubbles burst and the seed, lacking support, sinks, only to rise again as more bubbles cluster about it.

• **Remarks:** This is a really magical effect when well-timed to snaps of the fingers, which seemingly cause the seed to go up or down, but it is equally impressive as a straight scientific experiment, in which the action of the seed and the tiny bubbles of carbon dioxide are explained as they occur.

Glass to Glass

• **Effect:** Two small glasses are shown, one filled with water, the other empty. Both are set on a table and without touching either glass, the water is eventually transferred from one to the other.

• **Materials:** Two small glasses, some water, a strip from a paper towel and an object to serve as a stand, such as a box or another glass which can be inverted.

• **What To Do:** Set the full glass on the stand and the empty glass on the table be-

side it. Dip one end of the paper strip deep into the water and run the other end down to the empty glass. Immediately, the paper will begin to absorb water, which will gradually soak the entire strip. From then on, water will travel from the full glass to the empty until much of it has arrived in the lower glass.

• **WHAT HAPPENS:** Two scientific principles are found here; one, that of capillary attraction, whereby the water is drawn up through the fibres of the porous paper; the other, the principle of the siphon, in which the long end of a curved tube draws water from the short end.

• **REMARKS:** Since this experiment involves a very slow process, it is a good plan to start it long in advance of other demonstrations, coming back to it after a half-hour or more. By then, it will have reached an intriguing stage, fully illustrating the scientific principles at work.

The Floating Coin

• **EFFECT:** A small coin is placed in a glass of water and to the surprise of the onlookers it floats there. Then, to prove that it is really metal and that it has defied a natural law, the coin is given a slight downward push, and it sinks to the bottom of the glass.

• **MATERIALS:** A small foreign coin composed of a light aluminium alloy. A glass of water.

• **WHAT TO DO:** Test your coin to see that it is light enough for the experiment. Take it at the very tips of thumb and finger, placing it absolutely flat on the water. Release the coin and if it floats, you can proceed to perform the same feat publicly.

After floating the first coin, more may be floated in the same manner, all at the same time. To sink a coin, tap it near one side, so that water comes up over the edge, and it will slide beneath the surface. Fish it out and dry it, and it can be floated again.

• **WHAT HAPPENS:** Due to contact with the air, the molecules composing water form a thin film which is scientifically termed "surface tension." This can support small objects which normally would sink, provided care is taken not to disturb the tension. Study the coin as it floats and you will see how it presses down into the water as though sustained by an invisible film.

Steel that Floats

- **Effect:** After demonstrating that light metal can float, the next step is to prove that steel will do the same. This is done by using a small needle as a miniature bar and floating it on water.
- **Materials:** A thin needle, a dinner fork, a cigarette paper, and a glass of water.
- **What To Do:** With thumb and finger rest

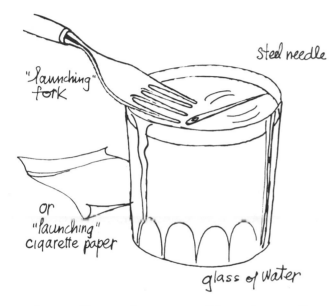

"launching" fork

or "launching" cigarette paper

steel needle

glass of water

the needle on the water. Often the needle will float. If not, dry the needle, set it across the prongs of the fork and lower it evenly into the water. Another way is to put the needle on the cigarette paper and float the paper. When it becomes soggy and sinks, the needle will float serenely on the surface.
- **What Happens:** The surface tension of the water sustains the steel needle. Fork and paper are merely launching devices.

Always North

- **Effect:** A needle, floating in a glass of water, begins a slow, steady, mysterious turn, finally pointing in a fixed direction.

Glass of Water

North!

Magnetized Needle

- **Materials:** A needle, a magnet, and a glass of water.
- **What To Do:** First, magnetize the needle with the magnet. Next, float the needle as described in the previous experiment. It will begin to turn of its own accord, finally remaining fixed.
- **What Happens:** The needle, being magnetized, acts like the needle of a compass, turning until it points due north.

Magnetic Plastic

- **Effect:** A ping-pong ball is dangled on the end of a strong thread or light string and is flipped into a stream of water descending from a running tap. The ball clings there as though magnetized, requiring a strong pull to break the contact.
- **Materials:** A ping-pong ball, some adhesive tape, a foot of thread or string, and a handy tap.
- **What To Do:** Fix the ball to the end of the string, turn on the water to form a steady

stream and flip the ball into it from a few inches away, while you hold the upper end of the string. Not only will the ball stay with the string at an angle, you can draw the ball up the stream almost to the tap.

of the water as you draw the ball upward, the air pressure is still stronger, as the experiment proves.

The Strong Napkin

• EFFECT: A paper napkin is twisted like a rope, and someone is asked to pull the ends and make it break. The napkin proves too strong to give way to an ordinary tug, and some large napkins will not break at all. That is, not unless you know the trick, in

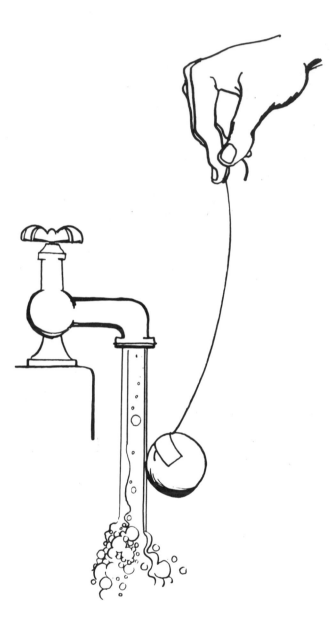

• WHAT HAPPENS: The water, streaming around one side of the ball, exerts less pressure than the air which surrounds the other side. Even though you can feel the resistance

which case you can snap the napkin easily.

• MATERIALS: Some paper napkins and a glass of water.

• WHAT TO DO: Twist each napkin rope-wise and let people try to break them with a pull. Meanwhile, dip your fingers in the water and apply it to the centre of your napkin while you are twisting the napkin tighter. A few dips may be needed, but once the water has permeated the napkin, it will snap easily.

• WHAT HAPPENS: Water tends to reduce the paper to the original pulp from which it was formed, thus weakening the fibres so that they will readily come apart. In this case, the early stages of the process are sufficient.

• REMARKS: By dampening the napkin unnoticed, you can keep people puzzled regarding the secret, and they will credit you with an actual feat of strength.

Topsy-Turvy Eggshell

• EFFECT: An eggshell is floated in a tall glass of water, then gradually pushed below the surface. As it starts to sink, the shell is

given a slight flip by the finger, and it turns over before it reaches the bottom of the glass, where it rests upside down.

• MATERIALS: The half-shells of a newly opened egg. (The shell from a fried or scrambled egg will do.) Two tall glasses, two long spoons or forks.

• WHAT TO DO: Take the large end of the egg and note the little air pocket inside it, formed by the lining of the egg. This must be intact for the experiment to work. Float that half-shell in a glass and gradually push it under water, pretending to flip it with your finger as it sinks. The flip is really unneeded as the egg will automatically turn upside down before it reaches the bottom of the glass.

Let someone else try it with the small end of the egg and the other glass. The shell, once filled with water, will sink straight down without turning over. The shells can be fished out with spoon or fork and the experiment repeated. Always, you seem to have the magic touch that makes your half-shell turn over, while the other half-shell won't respond, as it has no air pocket.

• WHAT HAPPENS: The half-shell of an egg is almost buoyant enough to float and the tiny air pocket is sufficient to bring the bottom end up, just as a sinking ship is apt to turn turtle, due to the air remaining in it. But the big end of the egg still is not quite light enough to float, hence you pretend to flip it over, as if you were performing a trick instead of a scientific experiment. This turns a simple test of buoyancy into a minor mystery.

• REMARKS: Be sure that the air pocket is intact before you start; otherwise, you will need another eggshell. After the experiment, you can puncture the film with your finger, so that if anybody wants to test your half-shell, it will no longer work. If you are asked to repeat the effect, get two more glasses and another egg. Then you can work it just as before—with the big end of the new egg—while three other people try unsuccessfully to make a half-shell turn over while it sinks.

Pepper and Salt

• **EFFECT:** A sizable pinch of salt is poured on a sheet of paper. The salt is then sprinkled generously with nearly the same amount of pepper. People are asked to estimate how long it would take to separate the pepper from the salt. Estimates may vary anywhere from an hour to a year; hence onlookers will

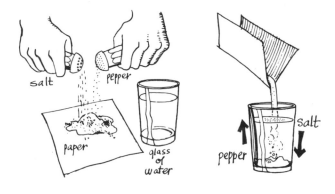

be amazed when they see it done in a fraction of a second.

• **MATERIALS:** Shakers or containers of pepper and salt. A sheet of paper. A glass of water.

• **WHAT TO DO:** Pour some salt on the paper, then add some pepper; or mix them alternately if preferred. Propound the question; then, to show how rapidly the separation can be made, simply dump the mixture into the water. The salt promptly sinks, leaving the pepper on the surface.

• **WHAT HAPPENS:** The grains of salt, being heavier than water, naturally sink and begin to dissolve. The flakes of pepper, being much lighter than water, naturally float. Hence the separation is completely automatic and almost instantaneous, fulfilling the stated requirements. It is simply a demonstration of the specific gravity of the two items, pepper and salt.

• **REMARKS:** On Page 98, you will find a similar effect under the heading of "Salt and Pepper," in which the same two substances are rapidly separated by an entirely different process. These experiments can be alternated; or, if asked to repeat one, you can use the other, adding a fresh surprise.

Lifting an Ice Cube

• **EFFECT:** Drop an ice cube in a glass of water, give someone a piece of string and ask him to lift the cube from the glass, using only the string and without touching either the glass or the ice cube with his hand. Apparently, he must loop the string around the ice cube, which proves impossible. So you demonstrate the easy way, whereby you lift the cube with the string on your first try!

• **MATERIALS:** A glass of water, an ice cube, a piece of string several inches long, and a shaker full of salt.

• **WHAT TO DO:** Drop one end of the string so that it forms a coil, resting on the ice cube. Sprinkle salt on the cube and wait while the ice melts slightly and then refreezes, imbedding the coiled string in it. Lift the string, and the ice cube will come up with it, enabling you to remove it from the glass.

• **WHAT HAPPENS:** The salt lowers the freezing point of the ice and causes it to melt. (That, incidentally, is the reason why a salt-water bay won't freeze over when a fresh-water lake will.) After the salt dissolves, the ice freezes again and grips the coiled string firmly enough to lift the ice cube from the glass.

Sink or Swim

• **EFFECT:** Two large drinking glasses are shown, each well filled with water. An egg is placed in the glass and sinks gracefully to the bottom, as a well-behaved egg should. Another egg is then placed in the second glass, but to everyone's amazement it floats serenely on the surface, apparently under some magical control.

As if that were not enough, another perplexing experiment may follow. Spectators are given the choice of either egg, and the one chosen is brought from the glass with a spoon, the other egg being similarly withdrawn, but laid aside. Water is poured from both glasses into a third and larger glass.

When the chosen egg is placed in this new container, it refuses either to sink or swim, but stays submerged halfway between the bottom and the surface, like a lurking submarine.

• **MATERIALS:** Two large glasses, two small eggs, and a spoon. A carton or package of salt. A still larger glass for the further experiment, and a pitcher filled with water. Instead of glasses, wide-mouthed jars may be used, the smaller ones of pint capacity, the larger jar a quart size.

• **WHAT TO DO:** Pour water into glass "A" until it is well filled, then leave it as it is. Pour nearly the same amount into glass "B,"

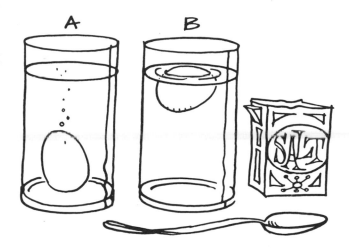

then add salt and keep stirring to form a strong saline mixture. The exact amount of salt is determined by testing the mixture with an egg. When the egg is floating nicely on the surface, remove the egg and dry it. All is then ready for presentation.

In working the experiment, place an egg in glass "A" and call attention to the way it sinks. Put the other egg in glass "B" and pronounce a "magic" word to make it float. The eggs can be removed and put in the opposite glasses, to show that both eggs are alike and that either will respond when you command it to float.

For the added experiment, remove the eggs

from glasses "A" and "B"; then pour water from those glasses into the larger glass, "C," until it is about half filled. Then place the chosen egg in "C" and keep adding water from "A" and "B" in small quantities until the egg finds a mid-point in the combined mixture.

• WHAT HAPPENS: Since the density of the fresh water in "A" is less than that of the egg, the egg naturally sinks. The addition of salt to the water in "B" forms a solution of greater density than the egg, which therefore is buoyed to the surface. Careful mixture of the fresh water and the salt solution in "C" will result in a liquid of the same density as the egg, which can be held at the mid-point.

• REMARKS: Coloured or tinted glasses may be used, so any difference in the appearance of the fresh water and the saline solution will not be observed. If only clear containers are available, avoid too strong a light. With containers of just the right proportions, the larger one, "C," can serve instead of a pitcher. Simply fill "A" and "B" from "C" beforehand; then proceed as described.

loose...   taut!   Not a drop spilled!

Anti-Gravity Handkerchief

• EFFECT: A handkerchief is draped over a tall glass, and the centre of the cloth is pushed downward, forming a fairly deep pocket. Water is then poured from a pitcher into the glass, soaking the centre of the handkerchief. There is nothing surprising about this; obviously, water should penetrate the cloth and fill the glass.

But what follows is extraordinary indeed. The wet handkerchief is drawn down outside the glass so that the centre is stretched across the mouth of the glass. Then the glass is inverted with the cloth still in place. Not only does the handkerchief stay there, so does the water. The handkerchief literally retains the water in the glass, defying the law of gravity!

• MATERIALS: A pitcher of water, a tall glass, and an ordinary handkerchief, which may be borrowed for the experiment.

• WHAT TO DO: Drape the cloth over the glass, pushing it well down in, so as to soak most of the centre when you fill the glass from the pitcher. Draw the cloth taut and press it firmly around the outer rim of the glass to prevent any leakage. Place one hand over the mouth of the glass and invert it with the other. Remove the lower hand and the water will stay, presumably proving that the handkerchief has anti-gravity propensities.

If the handkerchief is a small one, you can release it entirely, letting it remain as the sole support of the full load. With a large handkerchief, much of it can be wrapped about the glass and gripped by the upper hand; but if most of it is wet, it will adhere of its own accord. In that case, the upper hand can grip the glass itself, above the level of the handkerchief.

For the finish, place the lower hand beneath the mouth of the glass, press firmly, and reverse it back to normal. Remove the handkerchief and pour the water back into the pitcher to prove that all is fair.

• **WHAT HAPPENS:** Two scientific principles are involved in this intriguing experiment. Air pressure, working from the outside, forces the handkerchief against the glass, thus retaining the water inside. That would be nullified by any leakage, which in turn is prevented by surface tension, provided that the cloth is pressed tightly and evenly while the glass is kept at an exact level.

• **REMARKS:** Be careful with this experiment, as any slight miscalculation may result in leakage, although that may be counteracted by prompt adjustment of the handkerchief. Preliminary tests usually will insure this, but in presenting the experiment, it is always advisable to hold the glass directly above the pitcher. Then, if the water should suddenly escape, it will fall back where it belongs and the experiment can be attempted again, without admitting failure. Simply tell the spectators that they have seen what ordinarily happens; now, they should be prepared to witness something extraordinary.

The Spinning Eggshell

• **EFFECT:** Half an eggshell is placed near the rim of a large dinner plate, where it begins to spin, apparently of its own accord, running around and around the rim and climbing to the very edge, faster and faster, as though it could go on forever.

• **MATERIALS:** The half-shell from the large end of an egg, with its filmy air pocket intact. A dinner plate, preferably of the modern type with upward curving rim. A glass of water.

• **WHAT TO DO:** Moisten the plate around the rim. Hold the plate with thumb well

back, fingers below; then, with the other hand, set the eggshell on the opposite side. Tilt the plate slightly forward and either to left or right. The eggshell will then commence to spin in that direction. Only the slightest motion of the hand is needed to keep it spinning, not only rapidly but uncannily, on and on.

• **WHAT HAPPENS:** The slight cohesion caused by the moistened plate rim forces the shell to rotate in what becomes a demonstration of centrifugal force, as the shell seeks escape. Further tilting of the plate will increase the shell's speed, but such tilts can be all but imperceptible. With practice, such perfect control is possible that this will seem a feat of skilled jugglery rather than a simple scientific experiment.

• **REMARKS:** This interesting exhibition has been used to illustrate the double movement of the earth; namely, its rotation on its axis and its revolution around the sun. Any central mark of design on the plate can represent the sun, with the eggshell as the earth, each complete spin being a day, and the full trip around the plate being a year.

Upright Corks

• **EFFECT:** A few corks are dropped into a large bowl of water, where they float about on their sides. The aim of this experiment is to make the corks float upright, which just can't be done. That is, not until the demonstrator proves it can be—not just with one cork, but with seven!

• **MATERIALS:** Seven corks of the same size, all cylindrical in shape. A bowl or deep pan filled with water.

• **WHAT TO DO:** Let people try to float single corks end up. After they fail, stand all the corks on the table, with one surrounded by the other six. Lift the cluster and thrust it down into the water, so the corks become completely wet. Release them and they will float together, every one end up.

• **WHAT HAPPENS:** The water, penetrating

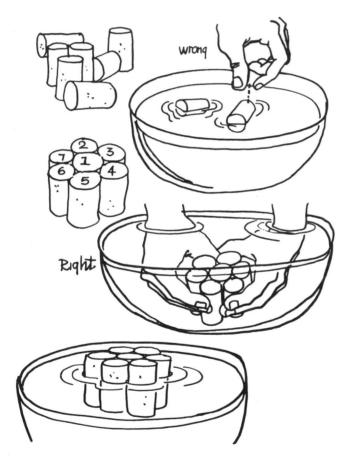

the corks by capillarity, causes them to cling together. Though each cork is in a state of unstable equilibrium, capillary cohesion re-

tains them in a united mass of greater width than height; hence they float in that position, all upright.

Strong Thread

• **EFFECT:** An empty coffee can is filled with water to give it weight. A length of thread is laid across the mouth of the tin, and the lid is pressed tightly in place. When someone tries to lift the can by the thread, the weight immediately breaks the thread, proving that it can't be done. But it can be done, as anyone who knows the secret can demonstrate on the next try.

• **MATERIALS:** A pound coffee can, preferably with a plastic lid, though metal will do. A spool of very fine cotton thread. A deep saucepan or small pail filled with water.

• **WHAT TO DO:** Pour water into the coffee can until it is almost full. Press the end of a length of thread beneath the cap, so that whoever tries to lift it will find the thread

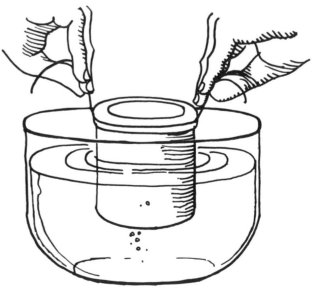

promptly breaks. When your turn comes, fix the thread in position, then put the coffee can into the saucepan of water. The coffee can will sink to the bottom, but when you pull on the thread, the can will come up easily. You can lift it several inches without any risk of breaking the thread, thus proving that you have accomplished the impossible.

• **WHAT HAPPENS:** This is a perfect demonstration of Archimedes' principle that a solid body immersed in water apparently loses weight equal to the amount of water it displaces. The coffee can, in effect, becomes so light that it can be lifted easily by the thread. After a few inches, the can will seemingly become heavier, so do not tax the string too far.

Air Versus Water

• **EFFECT:** Starting with two drinking glasses, one filled with water, the other empty, the water is poured back and forth from one glass to the other. This is quite simple; whenever the water enters a glass it forces out the air and the process is complete. But the demonstration becomes magical when it is done in reverse, pouring the air from one glass into the other and forcing out the water. Amazing though it sounds, it can be done!

• **MATERIALS:** Two small glasses, and a large bowl filled with water. Preferably, this should be a glass bowl, such as a fish bowl. A square-walled tank is even better, the purpose being to give spectators a full view of the experiment that follows.

• **WHAT TO DO:** Fill one glass with water and pour it back and forth from one glass to the other, remarking that the water forces

out the air. Then add that you will now pour the air from one glass to the other, forcing out the water. With that, invert the empty, or "air-filled" glass—which we will call Glass "A"—and push it straight down into the aquarium. The air will compress slightly, but will not escape, so you can point out that "A" is actually filled with air.

Next, dip the other glass—"B"—sideways into the tank, so that glass "B" becomes com-

pletely filled with water. You are then ready for the actual experiment. Invert glass "B" and bring it upward beside glass "A." Then tilt "A" sideways, so that its mouth comes just below the mouth of "B." The air escaping from "A" floats upward into "B," forcing water from "B" and filling it with air instead.

• WHAT HAPPENS: The water compresses the air in "A" when it is originally thrust mouth downward into the tank. Hence the air has no way of escape, because the bottom of the inverted glass "A" prevents the air from continuing upward and the water seals the rim of "A." This changes, however, when "A" is tilted. Water pressure forces air from "A" and the air expands, bobbing up toward the surface only to be trapped in glass "B."

There, the process reverses itself. Air pressure forces the water downward from "B" just as it originally resisted the water pressure in "A." Again, however, the air pressure is counteracted by the pressure of the water, which compresses the air to the same slight but noticeable degree that it did before. This time, it is the mouth of glass "B" that is sealed, retaining the air as long as "B" is kept completely inverted. Thus the air literally has been poured from glass to glass, though in an upward direction.

• REMARKS: Use of a fairly large bowl or glass tank enables observers to watch every detail of the experiment just as they might study marine life at an aquarium. However, the experiment is also visible when viewed from above.

The Hydrostatic Glass

• EFFECT: A sheet of paper is placed over the mouth of a glass of water, which is then inverted. The water stays in place and when

the paper is peeled away, it still remains in the glass, which is shown from every angle. But when the glass is held above a pitcher, the water gushes from the glass at command.

• MATERIALS: A drinking glass with fairly straight sides and a rather wide rim. A piece of fairly stiff transparent plastic cut to a size a trifle larger than the glass rim. A square sheet of paper, measuring a few inches more than the diameter of the glass. A wide-mouthed pitcher or a large, deep bowl.

• WHAT TO DO: Have the plastic disk lying beneath the square of paper near the edge of the table. Start by filling the glass with water from the pitcher. Pick up the paper

square and plastic disk together, with your thumb beneath and fingers above. Dip both in the pitcher so they adhere, though apparently you are merely moistening the paper.

Atmospheric Pressure Holds Disk in place

That done, place the paper carefully over the mouth of the glass and in so doing, adjust the disk to the rim of the glass. Press the paper with your free hand, which is kept flat and turn the glass completely over; then move the hand away, so the paper apparently holds the water in the glass. Actually, the plastic is performing that function, so the free hand next peels away the damp paper and the water seemingly stays in the glass by itself.

The glass is held with thumb at one side, fingers at the other, so for the climax, it is raised above the pitcher and the little finger presses the protruding edge of the disk downward, tilting the glass at the same time. The water immediately gushes down into the pitcher, carrying the disk with it.

• **What Happens:** The plastic disk is held in place by atmospheric pressure, while the paper square, being damp, merely adheres

to the disk until peeled away. Pressing the edge of the disk and tilting the glass combine to admit air and release the disk, which falls too fast to be observed amid the gush of water.

• **Remarks:** Certain types of prepared glasses may be utilized in this experiment. One type has an ornamental design which hides a $\frac{1}{16}$-inch hole bored in the side of the glass, about an inch up from the bottom. The left thumb is held over this hole when the glass is filled with water and is retained there until the time arrives to invert the glass. Then, the right thumb and fingers come straight up from below, taking the glass so that the right thumb supplants the left thumb. Later, by simply lifting the right thumb, air is admitted above the water level in the inverted glass.

Press edge of disk and... SplASH!

Hole admits air pressure at given moment

Other types of Glass

Another type of glass has the hole bored in the centre of the bottom. The glass is held in the left hand, which is palm upward, thumb at one side, fingers at the other, except the forefinger, which is directly beneath the hole in the bottom, pressing upward. The left hand holds the glass throughout the experiment, with the forefinger pressing constantly to prevent air from entering the hole until the final moment. Then, a trifling lift of the fingertip is sufficient to release the water and the disk with it.

Magic Milk

- **EFFECT:** An ordinary glass is shown full of milk. At command, the milk disappears by degrees until practically none is left. By giving another command, the milk returns in the same uncanny manner.
- **MATERIALS:** Two glasses, one rather tall,

the other shorter and narrower in diameter. A piece of very thin, pliable wire, 24-gauge being a good type. Some milk and some water.
- **WHAT TO DO:** Loop the wire around the smaller glass just below the rim, twisting one end to keep it in fixed position. Set the small glass in the large one and run the free end of the wire up over the rim of the large glass and down in back. Then form the free end into a loop slightly larger than your thumb.

Remove the small inner glass and pour a little milk into the large glass. Then put the small glass back in place and push it down until the milk is forced up between the small glass and the large one. Then pour water into the inner glass until it becomes heavy enough to stay down. With the glasses thus set, you are ready to perform the milk miracle.

Show the glass and state that it is full of milk, which it appears to be. Insert your thumb in the loop behind the outer glass and pull down slowly. This raises the inner glass and the milk subsides between the walls of the two glasses, as if vanishing by degrees. To make the milk return, slowly release the wire and the inner glass will settle to its original position, causing the "vanished" milk to reappear.
- **WHAT HAPPENS:** This trick works on the principle of a hydraulic elevator, in which a steel plunger forces water from a vertical pipe in order to descend, and rises when the water returns. Here, the inner glass serves as the plunger and its action depends on the scientific fact that milk, like other liquids, is not ordinarily compressible. Coming up and down between the walls of the two glasses, the milk completely surrounds the inner glass and being opaque, creates the illusion that the outer glass is filling or emptying as the case may be.
- **REMARKS:** Various glasses may have to be tried before finding two well suited to this experiment, but the effect is so good that it is worth the trouble. The inner glass should be quite plain so that it will look transparent when the milk is all at the bottom of the outer glass.

Instead of an inner glass, an actual plunger may be used, consisting of a cylinder of transparent plastic material. By drilling a small hole through the upper edge, a white thread can be used instead of the wire and enough milk can be put in the glass to cover the plunger entirely when the glass looks full. It can then be shown from all angles and from the top as well.

Roller Coaster

- **EFFECT:** A long, wide strip of paper is laid over the backs of some books, dipping down between them. Drops of water are started from the top and scoot down the dips and up again, like cars on a roller coaster.

When you show it to people, they will wonder how it could have come about. If you want, you can keep them indefinitely baffled regarding the label mystery.

- **MATERIALS:** A bottle with a label. Plenty of water.
- **WHAT TO DO:** First, immerse the bottle in warm water and soak off the label. Pour some water into the bottle and lay the bottle on its side. Roll the label around a pencil, draw the pencil free and carefully push the label into the bottle. After the label spreads out, shake the water from the bottle in little drips. The label will finally be left high and dry, fixed to the inside of the bottle.

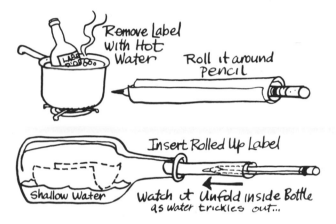

- **WHAT HAPPENS:** Once the rolled-up label is floating in the shallow water at the side of the bottle, the paper will absorb more water and therefore will tend to spread. From its rolled condition, it opens flat, floating on the water. As the water is shaken out, the label naturally settles and its damp side adheres to the bottom of the bottle so the label can be read through the glass.

- **MATERIALS:** A few books of different sizes, a long sheet of wax paper, some transparent tape, and a small glass of water. A saucer.
- **WHAT TO DO:** Arrange the books in order of size, from the largest to the smallest and stand them so the binding is upright. Run the wax paper over each book, letting it dip down very slightly in between. Set the saucer at the lower end.

When you let drops fall from the glass on the upper end of the paper, they will coast down and over the humps until they reach the saucer. If the waxed runway is at all unsteady, use the tape to fix its edges to the bindings of the books.

- **WHAT HAPPENS:** Since wax paper is impervious to moisture, water falling on it retains its spheroid form and naturally gravitates downward like raindrops on a windowpane. Such drops gather sufficient momentum to continue over slight rises in roller coaster fashion, turning a simple scientific experiment into an amusing diversion.

Label Inside Bottle

- **EFFECT:** Here is a real oddity, a bottle with a label on the inside instead of the outside!

Spread Away Matches

- **EFFECT:** Several matches are placed in a bowl of water, pointing outward like the spokes of a wheel. Without touching the matches or blowing them, they are spread to the sides of the bowl.

• MATERIALS: Some matches, a bowl of water, a piece of soap.

• WHAT TO DO: Arrange the matches spoke fashion in the water and dip the soap into the centre of the bowl. The matches will gradually spread away to the sides.

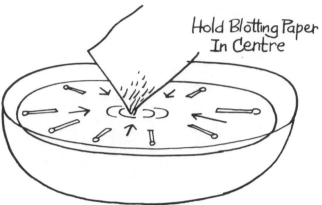

Hold Blotting Paper In Centre

Dip Soap in Centre of Water

• WHAT HAPPENS: The dissolving soap forms a film on the surface causing the floating matches to spread.

Magnetic Matches

• EFFECT: Several matches are floating at the sides of a bowl. Without touching them, they are brought to the centre.

• MATERIALS: Some matches, a bowl of water, a piece of blotting paper or a lump of sugar.

• WHAT TO DO: Dip the blotting paper or sugar lump into the centre of the bowl and

hold it there until the matches come together.

• WHAT HAPPENS: Water is drawn up by the blotting paper or sugar lump, due to capillary attraction. This, in turn, brings the matches to the centre of the bowl. A good follow-up to the "Spread Away Matches."

The Mysterious Diver

• EFFECT: A medicine dropper partly filled with water is floating upright in a tall jar of water covered with a sheet of rubber. At command, the improvised diver sinks to the bottom of the jar, then returns to the surface, or even wavers at the halfway mark.

• MATERIALS: A medicine dropper, a tall jar well filled with water, a sheet of rubber, which can be cut from a toy balloon, and a rubber band.

• WHAT TO DO: Dip the medicine dropper in the water and press the rubber bulb so the dropper is partly filled. Test the dropper in the jar and if it starts to sink, eject a few drops from it until finally it floats with the top of the bulb almost submerged.

Now, cap the jar with the sheet of rubber and fix the rubber band around the edges, so the jar is airtight. Push the rubber downward with your finger and the upright dropper will sink. Relax pressure and it will rise again. Time this to your commands so it seems to respond to them, even floating halfway if so ordered.

• **WHAT HAPPENS:** You have prepared a scientific device known as a "Cartesian Diver." The downward pressure on the rubber forces water up into the bottom of the diver, compressing the air above it, producing the effects of sinking, suspension, and floating according to the degree of the pressure.

• **REMARKS:** Many antique "divers" were made in the form of little figures which were termed "Bottle Imps" and which excited awe on the part of observers who witnessed this experiment a few centuries ago, when all science seemed like real magic.

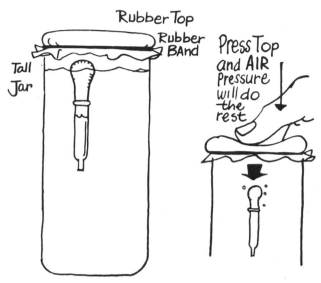

Rubber Top
Rubber Band
Tall Jar

Press Top and AIR Pressure will do the rest

Acoustrix

Tricks Involving Acoustics

The Singing Glass

• **EFFECT:** The prongs of a table fork are clicked with the thumb and fingernails. The hand is then stretched toward a drinking glass and a long, singing sound is drawn from it.

• **MATERIALS:** A fork, a glass, and a table.

• **WHAT TO DO:** Click the prongs of the fork sharply enough to gain a faint, responding note from the metal. Meanwhile, reach toward the glass and as your hand nears it, press the handle of the fork against the table with your other hand. The result is a strong, resonant sound, which you pretend to draw from the glass with the tips of your thumb and fingers, timing the action to the continuation of the sound.

• **WHAT HAPPENS:** Clicking the prongs causes vibrations that are scarcely heard because they take effect on only a very limited amount of the surrounding air. But when the handle is applied to the table they carry through the entire fork and the table itself becomes a sounding box that sets off still more vibrations. That is one factor, and for another, the greatly amplified sound is difficult for the ear to locate, so when you pretend to draw it from the glass, people will be positive that they really heard it come from that source.

• **REMARKS:** If you have trouble clicking the fork prongs with your fingernails, try clicking a small coin against them.

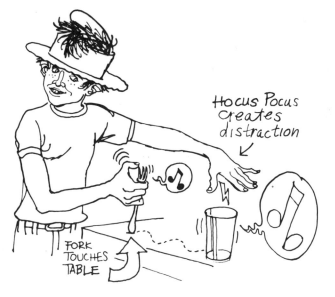

Hocus Pocus creates distraction

FORK TOUCHES TABLE

Big Ben

• **EFFECT:** Of course you have heard of Big Ben, the 13-ton bell that strikes the hours in the clock tower above the famous Houses of Parliament in London. But have you ever heard Big Ben? If not, here is your chance to prepare a simple device which will amaze your friends by reproducing the **distant** strokes of Big Ben. When they press two wires to their ears, they will hear the powerful *dong—dong—dong—*in a most realistic fashion.

• **MATERIALS:** A length of thin wire, measuring 3 to 4 feet. A large serving spoon.

• **WHAT TO DO:** Tie the spoon in the centre of the wire by forming a single knot there. Twist the ends of the wire together and put the joined end over your head so it comes in back of your ears. That will enable you to

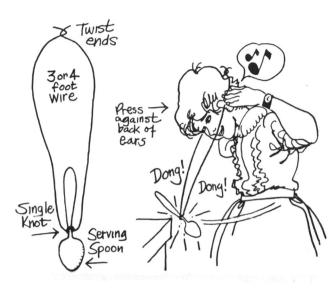

press your forefingers against the wire so that the wire is close against your ears.

Now, swing the spoon forward so it strikes the edge of a table. At each contact, you will hear the stroke of a great bell resembling Big Ben. Once you have it working to your own satisfaction, let your friends try it. If you want, you can swing the spoon for them, letting them count the clock strokes.

• **WHAT HAPPENS:** Most spoons are practically chimes in miniature, but their strokes are so light that their tones are lost. By using the wire as a conductor, the sounds are carried directly to the listener's ears and are thereby magnified to the tolling of a great bell.

The Dissolving Coin

• **EFFECT:** A large coin is placed beneath a handkerchief which is held above a glass con-

taining a small quantity of water. Anyone drops the coin into the glass, and everyone hears it land there. But when the handkerchief is drawn away, the coin is gone, apparently dissolved.

• **MATERIALS:** A drinking glass, preferably with a rather narrow bottom. A large coin and a plain glass disk of the same size. A small watch crystal may do, otherwise the disk must be cut from a piece of glass. A thick handkerchief.

• **WHAT TO DO:** Lay the handkerchief loosely on a table and hide the glass disk in its folds. Show the drinking glass, pour a little water into it, and have someone hold it. Exhibit the coin in your left hand, pick up the handkerchief with your right hand, and drape it over the coin. In so doing, grip the glass disk through the cloth with your right hand and extend it for the person to hold above the drinking glass. He thinks he is gripping the coin, but actually he has the glass disk. Have him drop the supposed coin into the glass, then pull away the handkerchief. To his surprise, the coin will be gone.

• **WHAT HAPPENS:** The tinkle of the falling disk makes everyone think that the coin has been dropped into the glass. Since the disk itself is glass, it remains unseen at the bottom of the drinking glass when the handkerchief is removed. Meanwhile, you drop the real coin into your pocket.

• REMARKS: Scientifically, this is an experiment in acoustics, as the clink of the disk is the factor that convinces people that the coin was really dropped into the glass. But to bolster the acoustical deception, other factors are brought into play. First, optics, for in looking at the supposedly empty glass, people actually see the disk but take it to be part of the glass itself. This illusion can be heightened by lifting the drinking glass almost to eye level, so that observers look through the side, instead of directly downward.

Finally, the scientific principle of adhesion can be used to advantage. To convince everyone that the coin has really vanished, you can pour the water from the glass. But the disk, having become completely moistened in its fall, adheres to the bottom of the glass, which can even be shaken to get rid of the last few drops. Later, the handkerchief can be used to wipe the glass dry; then the disk is taken away in the folds of the cloth.

Note: When using a very large coin or medal, the lens from a middle-sized flashlight can be used as the glass disc needed in this experiment.

Clink-Away Coin

• EFFECT: A coin is placed beneath a handkerchief and dropped into an empty glass. A rubber band is then fixed around the rim of the glass so that the coin cannot possibly escape. Anyone can hold the glass and then take away the handkerchief, to find the coin gone!

• MATERIALS: A tall drinking glass, a coin and a thick handkerchief. A rubber band, in the left coat pocket.

Tilted glass under cover

Coin Hits Side of Glass + Falls into Hand

• WHAT TO DO: Show the coin, put it beneath the handkerchief and hold it through the cloth with your right hand. Set the glass in your left hand and put it beneath the handkerchief, saying that you will drop the coin into the glass. Tilt the glass at an angle and let the coin fall so that it hits the outside of the glass with a resounding clink. It then drops into your left hand, which retains it.

Put the glass on the table with your right hand, with the handkerchief still covering the glass. Put your left hand into your coat pocket and drop the coin there. Bring out the rubber band and gird it around the rim of the glass, handkerchief and all. Anyone can then remove the handkerchief and find that the coin has apparently vanished from the glass.

• **WHAT HAPPENS:** In this case it is all acoustics. The coin clinks on the outside of the glass instead of the inside. If done properly —and it does require a bit of practice— everyone will suppose that the coin is still in the glass, the result being a really baffling climax.

HIDE COIN & PICK UP RUBBER BAND

Aeromagic

Magic Involving Aerodynamics

Lift the Book

• **EFFECT:** A large, heavy book is lying on a table. By simply blowing beneath the book, it is lifted upward a few inches. If a smaller book is set on top, the lower book can be lifted far enough for the upper book to slide off.

• **MATERIALS:** A large, fairly heavy book, a smaller book, a rubber balloon, preferably a long one, and some drinking straws.

• **WHAT TO DO:** Lay the heavy book on the table and to demonstrate what you intend to do tilt the near end with your left hand, stating that you can "lift the book like this by merely blowing under it." Have the balloon in your right hand and place it beneath

the book, but with the neck extended your way, so it still projects when you replace the book on it.

Stoop to the table and blow air into the balloon. As it inflates, it will lift the book. If the neck is not long enough, insert three or more soda straws in a cluster and roll the neck back to make it nearly airtight. Then blow through the straws to inflate the balloon.

• **WHAT HAPPENS:** This experiment shows the expansive power of air pressure. On a miniature scale, it is like inflating an automobile tyre and watching it lift the entire car. It takes an air pump to do that, but your lung power can lift a book—and more.

• **REMARKS:** Adding another book on top and having it slide off is simply a variant of this experiment, as lifting the lower book is essential in each case.

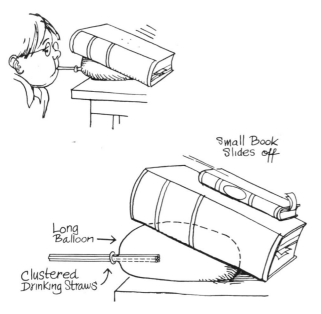

Small Book Slides off

Long Balloon →

Clustered Drinking Straws ↑

Strange Spheres

• **EFFECT:** Two ping-pong balls are suspended from the ends of a thread, so that they hang an inch apart. A person blows between the two balls to send them farther apart, but instead they come inward and bang together.

• **Materials:** Two ping-pong balls, two feet of thread, some mending tape and a drinking straw.

• **What To Do:** Tape each ball to an end of the thread and hold the centre so they dangle as described. Give your friend the straw so that he can blow exactly between the ping-pong balls from a distance of a few inches. Instead of being repelled, they will be attracted, as though by some magical power.

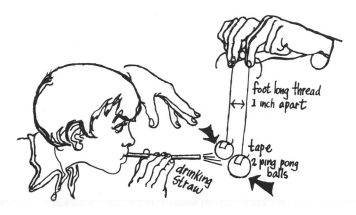

• **What Happens:** The air current directed between the ping-pong balls reduces the intervening air pressure. Stronger pressure from the far sides promptly pushes the dangling spheres together.

• **Remarks:** You can test this yourself by extending two rulers side by side from a bookshelf, with the inner ends held down by books. Hang the thread over the rulers so the balls dangle evenly below. A straw is not needed in the experiment, if you blow carefully between, but it will direct the current more effectively.

Chameleon Balloons

• **Effect:** A red toy balloon, fully inflated, is held in the left hand. The right hand

brushes the red balloon with a blue handkerchief. Instantly, the balloon's colour changes to blue.

• **Materials:** Two balloons, a red and a blue. A small rubber band. A blue handkerchief. A small black pin.

• **What To Do:** Push the blue balloon in through the neck of the red and inflate both together. Twist the rubber band around the neck of the blue balloon so no air escapes. Draw the neck of the red balloon wide and blow into it so it becomes larger than the blue balloon, with an air space between. Pressure is usually sufficient to keep the extra air in the outer (red) balloon; otherwise a rubber band must be put around its neck as well.

Fix the black pin in the hem of the blue handkerchief, letting a half-inch protrude. Exhibit the "red" balloon with the neck toward you, so people see the other end. Brush the red balloon with the handkerchief, letting the pin point puncture the rubber. Fragments of the red balloon will shrivel behind the blue balloon, which is shown intact, to prove the transformation complete.

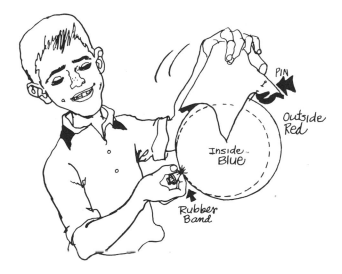

• **What Happens:** Since only the red balloon is punctured, it alone bursts. Scientifically, this demonstrates the outward effect of an explosion, as the inner (blue) balloon remains undamaged, due to the intervening air space. This differs from the blowout of an old-style automobile tyre, where a weakness in the outer casing, or shoe, could cause the inner tube to blow, since there was no air space between.

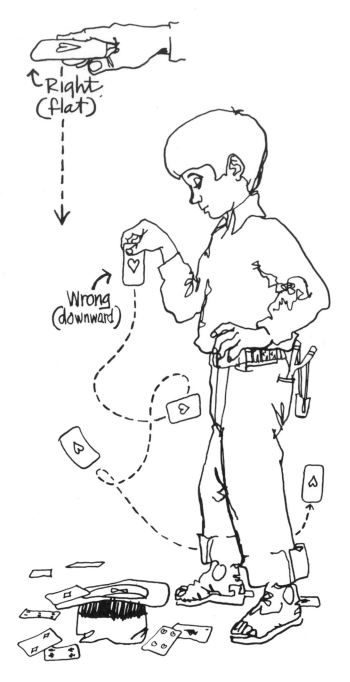

Crazy Cards

• **EFFECT:** People hold playing cards at shoulder level and try to drop them one by one into a hat that is lying brim upward on the floor. The cards scoot in all directions, missing the hat entirely, until they are dropped in a scientific way. Then they can't seem to miss.

• **MATERIALS:** A pack of playing cards and a hat.

• **WHAT TO DO:** Lay the hat on the floor and hold a card pointing downward above it, telling people to drop cards in the hat if they can. After they have watched their cards flutter away from the hat, hold a card perfectly flat, thumb at one side, fingers at the other, and release it. The card will float gracefully and evenly down into the hat.

• **WHAT HAPPENS:** This is really an experiment in aerodynamics, the air forcing the pointed cards into a spin, much like an unbalanced aeroplane wing. When held flat, the cards offer resistance similar to a parachute, hence the descent is evenly retarded.

• **REMARKS:** If dropped side downward, the cards will spin sidewise instead of endwise, missing the hat in either case.

Metal and Paper

• **EFFECT:** A metal coin and a small disk of paper are held at an equal distance above a table. Both are dropped, and the coin hits the table with a solid clank while the paper is still fluttering downward. Nobody is surprised, because they assume that the heavy coin *should* fall faster than the light paper. But when coin and disk are dropped a second time, both fall at exactly the same speed and reach the table simultaneously.

• **MATERIALS:** A coin, such as a florin. A disk of paper cut to a size slightly smaller than the coin.

• **WHAT TO DO:** First, hold the coin in one hand, the paper in the other and drop them side by side. The coin will reach the table well ahead of the disk. But the next time, hold the coin flat and set the disk on it, making sure that no edge of the paper protrudes. Drop the coin and the paper with it. Both will reach the table together.

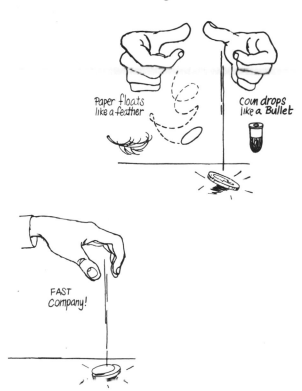

Paper floats like a feather

Coin drops like a Bullet

FAST Company!

• **WHAT HAPPENS:** It is a law of physics that all objects fall at the same velocity, regardless of their weight. Air resistance is the actual factor that retards the light paper more than it retards the heavy metal. By letting the paper disk ride along with the coin, such resistance is nullified and both fall at identical speed.

• **REMARKS:** This principle has been demonstrated by placing a bullet and a feather in a long, transparent tube from which the air is pumped and the tube then sealed to create a vacuum. When the tube is tipped one way and then the other, bullet and feather fall together, since there is no air to offer resistance. The simple experiment with coin and paper disk produces the same result without special equipment.

Blowing Through a Bottle

• **EFFECT:** Blowing out a candle is simple indeed, provided that there is nothing in the way. But suppose you hold up a bottle between yourself and the candle and then try to blow out the candle flame. That should be difficult, but you proceed to do it quite easily. Yet when anyone else tries it, the result is total failure.

• **MATERIALS:** A candle and candlestick. Two bottles, one with rounded corners, the other with square corners. Instead of bottles, metal or cardboard containers may be used; but they must meet the same specifications: One with rounded corners; the other with square corners, though the slighter the difference, the better.

• **WHAT TO DO:** Light the candle and hold the bottle with the rounded corners in front of it. Blow hard against the bottle and the candle will be extinguished. Ask some other person to try it, giving him the bottle with the square corners. No matter how hard he blows, the candle won't go out.

• **WHAT HAPPENS:** With a rounded bottle, the air currents separate, follow the curve of the bottle and converge beyond it, continuing on to extinguish the candle flame. It is a

simple experiment in aerodynamics, demonstrating the tendencies of air currents and illustrating how streamlining is of aid to aircraft in lessening air resistance.

With a square-edged bottle, the opposite holds true. The harder you blow, the more it

resists. The air currents divide, but simply dissipate off to the sides, taking no effect beyond the squared corners which deflect them. So your success, as opposed to your friends' failure, is entirely dependent upon your use of the rounded bottle.

• **REMARKS:** With a perfectly round bottle and another absolutely square, the demonstration is excellent from a scientific standpoint, but almost too obvious to provide real mystery. By testing various bottles, it is

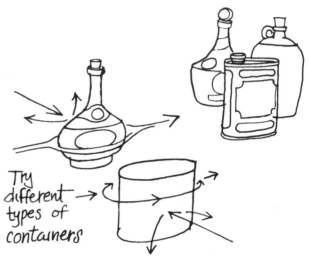

Try different types of containers

possible to obtain two of similar appearance, yet quite different where results are concerned. Just a slight rounding of the corners may enable the experiment to work, while too broad a surface may prove a handicap even if curved.

Some metal containers are sufficiently rounded to give good results, while most cardboard cartons, being square-edged, just won't work at all. There are, however, some oval-shaped bottles and tin containers that have two-way possibilities. Blow at them broadside and the candle won't go out; but turn them so the narrow sides are in line with the flame, and the air currents gain their needed flow. All this is worthy of scientific test.

A Surprising Lift

• **EFFECT:** A rubber balloon is inflated and pressed against the rim of an empty coffee can. The demonstrator states that he will lift the balloon and bring the can with it, without touching the can in any other way. After a few trials, he lifts the balloon and the can comes with it.

• **MATERIALS:** A toy balloon. An empty coffee can or similar container.

• **WHAT TO DO:** Inflate the balloon and press it against the mouth of the can. When you lift the balloon, the can fails to come

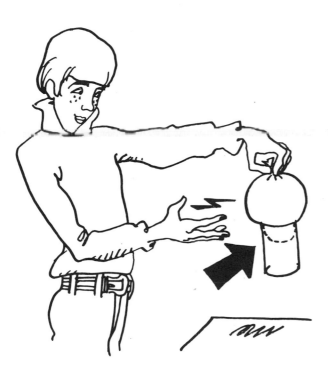

with it, so you let a little air out of the balloon and try again. Finally, let out enough air so the balloon is smaller than the diameter of the can.. Blow more air into the balloon and as you do so, lower the balloon into the can, so that as the balloon inflates,

it bulges against the inner wall of the can. Hold the neck of the balloon so no air escapes. Lift the balloon and the coffee can will come up with it.

• **WHAT HAPPENS:** The increasing air pressure tightens the balloon's grip against the can, much like an old-style inner tube pressing against the walls of an automobile tyre. Only a small amount of extra pressure is needed to lift the coffee can, so be sure to stop soon enough, as too much would mean a blowout!

• **REMARKS:** This is an excellent experiment to follow the "Hypnotized Balloon" on page 99, as people may think they are related, although the scientific principles are entirely different.

Blow the Book Down

• **EFFECT:** A heavy book is standing upright on a table. People are asked to blow it down, but when they try, they fail. Yet anyone who knows the right method can do it quite neatly.

• **MATERIALS:** A heavy book, a bottle filled with water, a string and a hook.

• **WHAT TO DO:** Hang the bottle from the string, which should be quite long, and may be hung from a doorway or a wall bracket. The table is placed just beyond, with the book standing on a level with the bottle, several inches from it. Start blowing on the bottle with short puffs and it will begin swinging, gaining momentum until it hits the book and knocks it down.

• **WHAT HAPPENS:** The bottle serves as a pendulum, which can easily be swung back and forth, since it is hanging freely. Repeated puffs of air build up its momentum until it has force enough to overturn the book, which would be impossible with a direct blow.

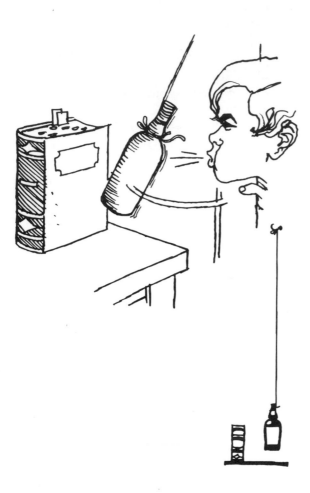

An Amazing Dart

• **Effect:** A person is given a needle and asked to throw it point first so it sticks in a dart board or a wooden surface. Naturally it fails, for it lacks the needed weight. Yet, by the simplest of procedures, it can be done.
• **Materials:** A large needle, a spool of thread, a wooden surface.
• **What To Do:** Thread the needle and cut the thread so that it measures several inches

each way. Throw the needle like a dart and it will find its target perfectly.
• **What Happens:** The trailing threads act

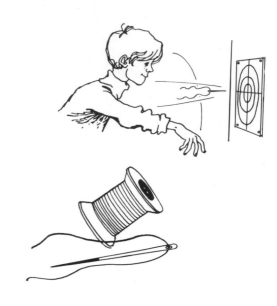

like the feathers on a throwing dart, steadying its flight quite effectively, even on this minor scale. An excellent study of aerodynamics.

Funny Funnel

• **Effect:** A funnel is inverted and its wide mouth is pressed downward upon an inflated toy balloon. The funnel is lifted, bringing the balloon with it.
• **Materials:** A toy balloon. A funnel.
• **What To Do:** Inflate the balloon until its diameter is greater than the mouth of the funnel. Place the mouth of the funnel against the balloon; then put the small end to your lips and draw in your breath. Slide the tip of your forefinger over the point of the funnel as you bring it from your lips. The balloon will remain fixed to the funnel.

• **WHAT HAPPENS:** The suction draws the balloon's surface into the funnel and the partial vacuum thus created is maintained by pressing the forefinger to the funnel's point. Often, a hard tug is necessary to pull the balloon free.

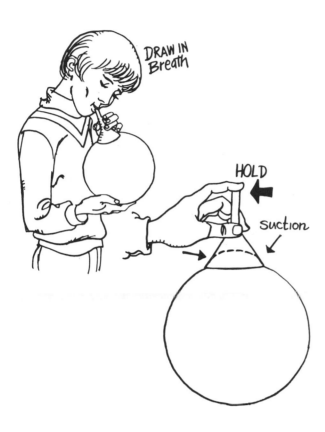

DRAW IN Breath

HOLD

suction

An Amazing Pincushion

• **EFFECT:** A pincushion is a very helpful item when you have a few loose pins lying about, but often a pincushion is so small that it is hard to find. A big one would be better, but it would be too heavy, unless you used something like a rubber balloon. Unfortunately, you can't stick pins into a rubber balloon. Or can you?

So saying, you blow up a toy balloon. Then, reminding your audience that anything is possible with magic, you speak the mystic word, "Science!" and jab the pin into the balloon. Does the balloon burst? Of course not! You jab another pin into it and then a few more, proving that a balloon makes the best of pincushions.

• **MATERIALS:** A rubber balloon. Several thin pins, preferably the type with large, coloured heads. A roll of plastic tape.

• **WHAT TO DO:** Inflate the balloon and affix little squares of plastic tape to it. Stick each pin through the centre of a dab of tape and to your own amazement, the balloon will not burst. Do the same with the other squares until you literally have a balloon serving as a pincushion. You then remove the pins, one by one, and still more amazing, the balloon still remains intact.

• **WHAT HAPPENS:** The adhesive substance on the tape acts like a self-sealing automobile tyre, adhering to the pin as it is pressed inward. When the pin is removed, the adhesive is forced outward by the air pressure from within the balloon, automatically sealing the tiny pinhole.

• **REMARKS:** The balloon can be deflated, then blown up again, and the patches will still hold, provided they were neatly affixed to start. Also, they hold better if the balloon is only partly deflated. This raises other possibilities where presentation is concerned, namely:

By inflating the balloon beforehand, then applying the patches and letting out most of the air, you will be all set to do the "pincushion" experiment without letting anyone in on its secret. Simply blow up the balloon without calling attention to its patches, and then push the pins into their centres, as though jabbing them hit or miss.

Nobody will see the patches if you stand several feet away, and if you use a balloon with a colourful design, you can put the patches in spots where they won't even be noticed at close range. Blow up the balloon, rub your hand over it in a mysterious manner and then jab the big-headed pins into your impossible pincushion and watch how the observers react!

Incidentally, rubbing the balloon in a mysterious fashion is more scientific than magical. It enables you to tell if any patches are a trifle loose. If they are, be sure to smooth them before jabbing pins into their centres.

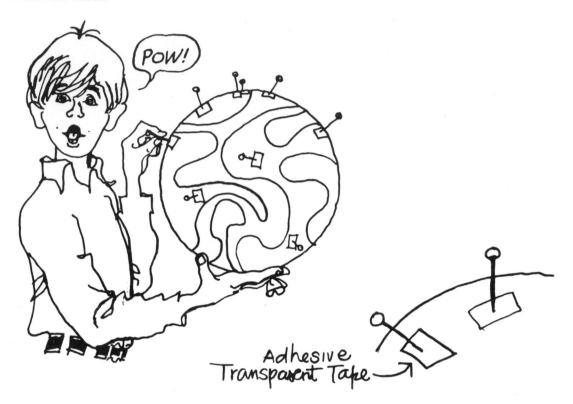

Adhesive Transparent Tape

Bring Them Together

• **EFFECT:** Two long strips of newspaper are held in each hand and dangled side by side a few inches apart. They are held edge forward, so they are actually broadside to each other. The dangling ends are then brought together in a most surprising way; namely, by trying to blow them apart!

• **MATERIALS:** Two long strips of newspapers, a few inches wide.

• **WHAT TO DO:** Hold the papers evenly and keep them directly in front of your body, a few inches apart, with your hands just below shoulder level. Remark that if you blow straight down between, the dangling ends should fly apart. However, through sheer wizardry, you will make them come together instead. Blow hard and steadily and the ends of the strips will be drawn together.

• **WHAT HAPPENS:** Blowing downward puts air in motion between the strips and thereby reduces the air pressure in that area. However, the atmospheric pressure which is all around us still functions as usual. It closes in from the outside and forces the ends of the paper strips together. Hence the action that seems mysterious is due to a simple scientific principle.

• **REMARKS:** This experiment is excellent in conjunction with "Weird Paper Strips" described on page 102. There, the paper strips behave just the opposite, being charged with static electricity. After their charge wears off, you can bring them together by blowing between them.

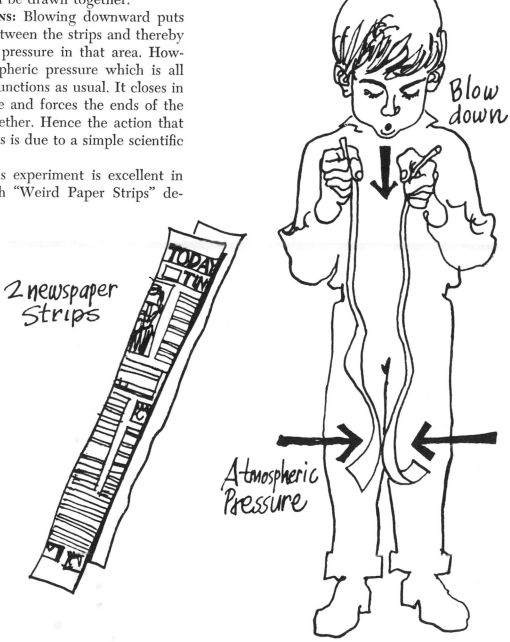

2 newspaper Strips

Blow down

Atmospheric Pressure

Arithmetrix

Tricks Involving Arithmetic

Apple, Egg, and Orange

• **EFFECT:** An apple, an egg, and an orange are placed on the table with a plate of crackers. While the performer's back is turned, one person takes the apple, another the egg, and a third the orange, putting them out of sight.

Again facing the group, the performer gives a cracker to one person, two crackers to the second, and three to the third person. He then states that whoever took the apple is to take just as many crackers as he was given; whoever holds the egg is to take twice as many crackers as he was given; while whoever has the orange is to take four times as many crackers as he was given.

All this is also done while the performer's back is turned. At this point, he has no idea as to which persons took the apple, egg, and orange. But when he faces them again, he

immediately points out all three persons correctly.

• **MATERIALS:** An apple, an egg, an orange, and a plate containing exactly 24 crackers. Other items may be used instead, as will be specified later. Also a special key list.

• **WHAT TO DO:** Prepare a typed or written key list which bears six numbers and six words, namely: Lancelot, Deacon, Canoe, Leopard, Romance, Korean. In each word, small letters are used, except for the vowels, which are in heavy capitals, thus:

1) l A n c E l O t
2) d E A c O n
3) c A n O E
4) l E O p A r d
6) r O m A n c E
7) k O r E A n

Have three persons take the apple, egg, and orange, as they decide among themselves. That done, give them crackers as described telling them how many more they are to take. That done, look at the plate and count the number of crackers left; then turn back again and secretly refer to your list.

For *one* cracker, you have "lAncElOt" and the position of the letters, A, E, O, signify that the first person has the apple (A), the second person the egg (E), and the third the orange (O).

For *two* crackers, dEAcOn signifies that the first person has the egg (E), the second the apple (A), the third the orange (O).

For *three* crackers, cAnOE tells that the first person has the apple (A), the second

Apple   Egg   Orange

24 crackers

Your secret code

94

the orange (O), and the third the egg (E).

For *four* crackers, lEOpArd shows that the first person has the egg (E), the second the orange (O), and the third the apple (A).

For *six* crackers, rOmAncE reveals that the first person has the orange (O), the second the apple (A), and the third the egg (E).

For *seven* crackers, kOrEAn tells that the first person has the orange (O), the second the egg (E), and the third the apple (A).

• WHAT HAPPENS: Scientifically, the experiment depends entirely upon a neat mathematical formula that leaves a different number of crackers for each arrangement of the apple, egg, and orange. So the trick works itself if you follow the routine to the letter.

• REMARKS: Other objects can be used instead of the apple, egg, and orange. For example, a card (for A), a pen (for E), a coin (for O). Instead of crackers, checkers, marbles, or paper clips will do, or even lumps of sugar. The working is the same in any case.

Magic Age Disks

• EFFECT: A person is handed five or six disks, all bearing numbers. He is told to pick out any disk on which he sees his age. That done, you immediately tell him what his age is. The experiment can be immediately repeated, using anyone else's age.

• MATERIALS: Disks bearing numbers as shown here. These can be copied on heavy paper or light cardboard.

• WHAT TO DO: Have the person lay aside each disk that shows his age. As he does, you note the centre number of that disk. Add them together mentally and the total will be the person's age.

Example: The person's age is 14 years. He sees it on the top disk at the right and the two disks in the middle. Their centre

numbers add $2 + 4 + 8 = 14$. Another person's age is 35. He sees it on the two top disks and the one at lower right. Their centre numbers add $1 + 2 + 32 = 35$.

• WHAT HAPPENS: The numbers 1, 2, 4, 8, 16, 32, form a geometric progression, in which they are increased by a constant factor, which in this case consists in multiplying each by 2. By taking them singly, or adding two or more together, it is possible to make any total from 1 to 63.

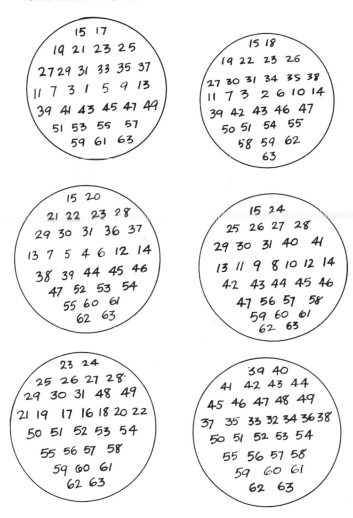

The disks illustrated here have been specially designed to include the various numbers required for each addition, so by picking out the disks with his age, a person will automatically provide you with the central "key" numbers. These will give you anyone's age up to 63 years.

• **REMARKS:** You can have a person think of anyone else's age and the disks will work just as well. For example, he might see the age of a three-year-old child on two top disks. (1 + 2 = 3). With anyone under 32 years old, you can work the experiment with the first five disks, retaining the one with the "key" number 32, as it will not be needed.

The Colours Tell

• **EFFECT:** A person notes his age on different disks, then turns the numbered sides down, yet you immediately tell his age.
• **MATERIALS:** Six "Magic Age Disks" cut from paper or cardboard of different colours, running in the order: Red, orange, yellow, green, blue, white.
• **WHAT TO DO:** Memorize the centre numbers according to the colour of the disks: 1 = red, 2 = orange, 4 = yellow, 8 = green, 16 = blue, 32 = white. Add them accordingly and the trick will work just like the "Magic Age Disks."

The Mystic Square

• **EFFECT:** A chart is divided into numerous small squares containing numbers from 1 to 25. Someone places a penny on the chart so that it covers the numbers on four squares. With a mere glance, you name the total of the squares covered by the coin. Finally, the coin is set so it covers five numbers in cross formation. This time you name the total without looking at the coin.
• **MATERIALS:** A specially numbered square as illustrated.
• **WHAT TO DO:** Use or trace the square shown. When someone covers the numbers

24	11	3	20	7	24	11	3	20	7
5	17	9	21	13	5	17	9	21	13
6	23	15	2	19	6	23	15	2	19
12	4	16	8	25	12	4	16	8	25
18	10	22	14	1	18	10	22	14	1
24	11	3	20	7	24	11	3	20	7
5	17	9	21	13	5	17	9	21	13
6	23	15	2	19	6	23	15	2	19
12	4	16	8	25	12	4	16	8	25
18	10	22	14	1	18	10	22	14	1

on four squares with a coin, you simply count diagonally from a corner of the group thus covered. Stop at the second square you reach and mentally subtract its number from 65. That will give you the total of the numbers on the covered squares.

Example: Squares with numbers 22, 14, 3, and 20 are covered, totalling 59. The second square diagonally away (in any direction) contains the number 6. This, subtracted from 65, gives you 59.

When five numbers are covered, the cross thus formed will always total 65. (Example: 3 + 17 + 9 + 21 + 15 = 65). So you simply call off "65" without even glancing at the chart. But make this your final call, as to repeat it might give away the system.
• **WHAT HAPPENS:** This chart is an elaboration of a mathematical device in which the numbers from 1 to 25 are grouped in a block measuring 5 by 5 to form what is known as a "Magic Square" where all rows add up to the same total, namely 65. Here, duplicate squares have been added to form a much larger group of interlocking "Magic Squares" which produce the mathematical effect as described.

Deceptive Dominoes

• **EFFECT:** A set of dominoes is spread on the table and people are invited to start with the Double-Six and add other dominoes as in a regular game. Before they start, you write a prediction on a slip of paper and put it in an envelope. After all the dominoes have been played, the end numbers of the row are noted, say One and Four. The message is opened and it bears the numbers "1" and "4"—a perfect prediction of the game's outcome!

• **MATERIALS:** A set of dominoes.

• **WHAT TO DO:** Beforehand, remove any domino from the set, making sure that it is not a "double" (as 6-6, 5-5, down to 0-0.) Note the number on that domino before you pocket it (in this case the 1-4) and write that as your prediction.

• **WHAT HAPPENS:** A neat mathematical principle is involved. A game of dominoes, if played to the finish, will wind up with the same end numbers; that is, the set will complete a full circuit. Few people realize this, however, as most games are blocked before the finish. The domino that you secretly remove is the one needed to complete the circuit, hence in this case it is your key to how the game will end.

• **REMARKS:** The illustration shows the game played out in full, with the "doubles" set crosswise and therefore having no effect upon the matching of the ends. After your first prediction, you can secretly return the 1-4 to the set and remove another, as the 0-3, using it as the key to a new prediction.

Electrix

Tricks with Electricity

Salt and Pepper

• **EFFECT:** Shake some salt onto a table or any convenient surface; then add a small amount of pepper so that the black flakes stand out sharply amid the white. The trick is to remove every flake of pepper, leaving only salt. It would take quite a while to pluck the pepper from the salt, flake by flake. But it can be done a lot faster, as the scientific magician promptly proves.

• **MATERIALS:** Shakers containing salt and pepper. A pocket comb, preferably rubber, though a plastic comb will do.

• **WHAT TO DO:** Shake out a fairly large quantity of salt. Then sprinkle pepper sparingly on the surface of the salt. The best way is to shake some pepper into the palm of the left hand; then, with the right thumb and forefinger, pinch some pepper flakes and strew them in the salt.

With all in readiness for the experiment, bring out the pocket comb and stroke it rapidly through your hair or rub it vigorously on your coat sleeve. Then carry it across the little pile of salt, and the flakes of pepper will fly up the comb, leaving the salt without a greyish speck in its entire surface.

• **WHAT HAPPENS:** The comb becomes charged with static electricity which attracts the light pepper flakes and clears them instantly from the salt. Some grains of salt will be attracted, too, but they can be plucked from the comb by the thumb and fingers, along with the pepper. The purpose

was to remove the pepper so a little salt won't matter.

• **REMARKS:** For a similar experiment, see

PLASTIC COMB

RUB COMB ON SLEEVE

"Pepper and Salt" on page 68. Though almost the same in effect, the scientific principle is entirely different, so one can be substituted for the other, thus surprising persons who think they already know the trick.

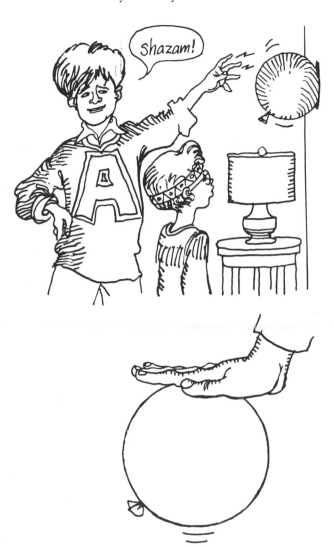

Shazam!

Hypnotized Balloon

• **EFFECT:** An inflated toy balloon adheres wherever it is placed, whether against the wall, the ceiling, or the palm of the downturned hand. Finally, at command, it drops to the floor and can be examined to prove that it is free from preparation.

• **MATERIALS:** A toy balloon, a rubber band. A piece of fur or wool cloth, though usually the coat sleeve will serve.

• **WHAT TO DO:** Inflate the balloon and twist the rubber band around its neck to prevent the escape of air. Rub the balloon against the coat sleeve or other specified material and place it against the wall, the ceiling—if it is low enough—and finally the downturned palm. By working it to the tip of the fingers, you command it to fall, which it does.

• **WHAT HAPPENS:** Rubbing the balloon charges it with static electricity, which causes it to cling to objects, as described. One hand can be used to place the balloon against the palm of the other hand and as the charge lessens, the balloon can be shaken free. If picked up immediately it will often adhere to the hand again.

• **REMARKS:** To turn this into a real mystery, have the balloon in another room, or step from sight with it, so you can rub the balloon and generate the electricity without anyone knowing it. People will then think that the balloon's behaviour is due to threads or to some sticky substance. This will leave them baffled when they examine the balloon later.

Contrary Balloons

• **EFFECT:** Two balloons are tied to the ends of a three-foot thread, which is held at the centre. Instead of hanging side by side, the balloons shy away from each other, rising at upward angles so that the thread forms an inverted V, with the balloons well apart. When the free hand is placed between the balloons, they swing down together, only to veer apart when the hand is drawn away. At last, they will come together.

• **MATERIALS:** Two balloons, a three-foot

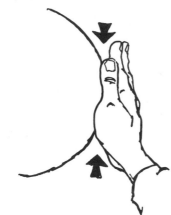

when two similarly charged objects are brought together, they repel each other, as in this case. The balloons naturally fly part, but when the hand is inserted, it attracts them both, seemingly bringing them together. Once the hand is removed, the balloons revert to their repulsion.

• **REMARKS:** This can simply be repeated until the static electricity has been reduced to such a minimum that the balloons hang together normally, which completes the demonstration.

Magic Wallpaper

• **EFFECT:** A piece of newspaper is placed against a wall and is given some long, steady strokes, as if to fix it there. This seems futile at first, but suddenly the paper remains in place. Other sheets can be hung in the same fashion, then peeled away, one by one, leaving no marks whatever.

• **MATERIALS:** A few sheets of newspaper, which can be torn into pieces of various sizes. A pencil.

length of thread, and a piece of fur or wool, or wool clothing.

• **WHAT TO DO:** Rub the balloons rapidly against the fur or wool and take the middle of the thread between the left thumb and fingers, extending the left hand at arm's length. The balloons will shy away; then come together when the right hand is thrust between them. This can be repeated a few times, until finally the balloons hang side by side.

• **WHAT HAPPENS:** Rubbing the balloons charges them with static electricity, which attracts uncharged objects, or vice versa. But

• **WHAT TO DO:** Hold the paper against the wall with one hand, press the pencil flat against it and stroke it hard and steadily until the paper stays there.

• **WHAT HAPPENS:** The paper becomes charged with static electricity and adheres to the wall as a result. This experiment works best in cool, dry weather, when the newspaper will stay fixed like actual wallpaper until the charge lessens. If no pencil is handy, double your fingers and rub the paper with your fingernails.

Sticky Paper

• **EFFECT:** Small sheets of paper are pressed against a person's back, a coat sleeve, or a trouser leg. The papers stick there magically.

• **MATERIALS:** Some pieces of newspaper. A pencil.

• **WHAT TO DO:** Use the pencil to rub each piece of paper against the wall until it stays there; then transfer the paper to the back, sleeve or trouser leg. Or the paper may first be placed against a person's back or sleeve and rubbed with the fingernails.

• **WHAT HAPPENS:** The rubbing process generates static electricity in the pieces of paper, causing them to stick to neutral or uncharged surfaces, as they do with the wall.

The Magnetic Pen

• **EFFECT:** A ball-point pen is passed above some bits of paper that are lying on a table. The pen immediately becomes magnetic, picking up the paper bits.

• **MATERIALS:** A plastic pen and some bits of paper.

• **WHAT TO DO:** Rub the pen rapidly and vigorously on your coat sleeve; then move it just above the papers and watch it pick them up.

• **WHAT HAPPENS:** Rubbing the pen on wool charges it with static electricity. It will then attract bits of paper, much as a magnet picks up steel or iron, though the charge is only temporary. A comb may be used instead of a pen for this experiment.

The Balanced Straw

• **EFFECT:** A drinking straw is balanced with nearly half its length extending from a table edge. A ball-point pen is moved beneath the straw which follows it back and forth and finally topples from the table, drawn by an unseen force.

• **MATERIALS:** A drinking straw and a plastic pen.

• **WHAT To Do:** Rub the pen briskly on your coat sleeve or some woollen surface. Bring it up beneath the straw and you will find a point where the straw will waggle back and forth when you move the pen to left or right. Raise the pen still higher and the straw will dip down to it, toppling as you pull the pen away.

• **WHAT HAPPENS:** Static electricity in the pen attracts the paper straw just as it would draw bits of paper. When approached from below or from the outer end, the straw will move sideways but will not topple as most of its weight is still on the table. Closer approach or actual contact enables the charged pen to draw the free end of the straw downward. Other rubber or plastic articles can be used instead of a pen, but it is a good plan to test them with a straw before working the experiment.

Move to Left + Right

Weird Paper Strips

• **EFFECT:** Two long strips of newspaper are held by the right thumb and fingers so that the lower ends of the strips dangle. But instead of staying together, the ends spread outward at a surprising angle.

• **MATERIALS:** Two long strips of newspaper. A pencil.

• **WHAT To Do:** Hold the strips side by side against the wall and stroke them forcibly with the side of the pencil. Then dangle the strips together and the lower ends will spread apart automatically.

• **WHAT HAPPENS:** Rubbing charges both strips with the same type of static electricity, in this case a negative charge. Objects so charged repel each other. Since the upper ends of the strips are held together, they cannot separate, and the action is confined to the lower ends, creating a most mysterious effect.

The Impossible Match

- **EFFECT:** A coin is set on its edge and a paper match is balanced on top of it. A drinking glass is inverted over both. The match is then removed from the coin, which still remains balanced, without touching the glass or moving it in any way.

Impossible? That's what everyone will say until you prove that it can be done!

- **MATERIALS:** A coin, a paper match, a glass, preferably of the goblet type, and a pocket comb.

- **WHAT TO DO:** Balance the match on the coin, bending the match slightly if necessary to make it rest crosswise. Cover it with the glass and state what is about to happen. When nobody believes it can happen, bring out the pocket comb. Stroke it through your hair or rub it on your coat sleeve and move it close to the glass. The match will fall off in the uncanniest way imaginable, leaving the coin still balanced on edge beneath the glass.

- **WHAT HAPPENS:** Static electricity, generated in the rubber or plastic comb, attracts the paper sufficiently to topple the match from the coin.

- **REMARKS:** Try this out to make sure you have it right. A goblet may be helpful, as it enables you to come closer to the match from

above. Balancing the coin on edge and the match across it, is a rather delicate demonstration in itself, making a nice buildup to the finale.

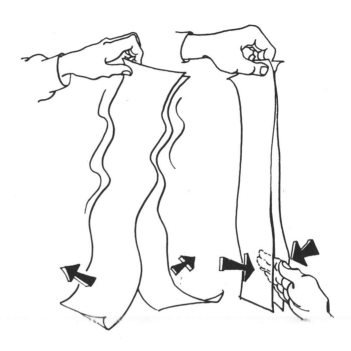

The Magnetic Hand

- **EFFECT:** Two paper strips are held by the right hand with the lower ends spread mysteriously apart. The left hand is brought up between them and the two strips are attracted to it, only to separate whenever the hand is lowered.

- **MATERIALS:** Strips of newspaper and a pencil.

- **WHAT TO DO:** Present this experiment as a follow-up to the "Weird Paper Strips." Rub and dangle the strips as described, and bring your free hand up between. It will draw the spread ends together.

- **WHAT HAPPENS:** The hand, being a neutral object, attracts the ends of the charged paper strips. Once it is lowered, the papers again repel each other and spread apart.

Magnetrix

Tricks Utilizing Magnets

Mystic Paper Clip

• **EFFECT:** A paper clip is dropped into a small, round plastic bottle which is filled with water. The stopper is put in the bottle, and the demonstrator places it behind his

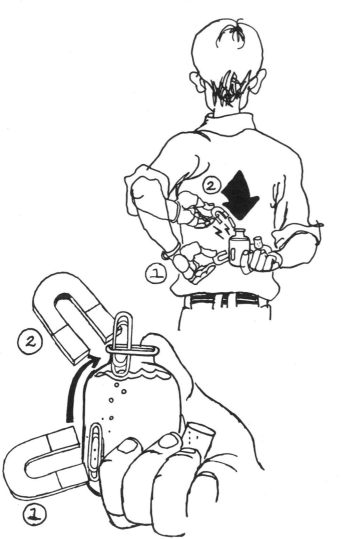

back. Soon he brings out the bottle, still corked, but with the paper clip lying loose in his hand beside it. Yet the water is still in the bottle.

• **MATERIALS:** A plastic bottle about one inch in diameter. A paper clip. A small magnet Some water.

• **WHAT TO DO:** Hold the magnet concealed in your right hand. After the clip has been put in the bottle and the stopper added, receive it with your left hand and place both hands behind your back. There, you keep the bottle upright, uncork it, and press the magnet against the side near the bottom. Draw the magnet up and the paperclip will come up with it, inside the bottle, attaching itself to the magnet as it emerges. Replace the stopper and pass out the bottle with your right hand, keeping the magnet in your left.

• **WHAT HAPPENS:** The intervening plastic has no effect upon the magnet's attraction of the steel paper clip, hence the removal of the clip from the bottle is practically automatic.

• **REMARKS:** A spectator can paste a label on the bottle and mark it with his initials to prove there is no exchange of bottles behind the performer's back. Use of a narrow bottle makes it impossible to bring out the paper clip with a finger without spilling water, so by keeping the magnet concealed, you can repeat the mystery, unless you prefer to reveal it as a scientific experiment.

Slippery Mucilage

• **EFFECT:** Some playing cards are held in a small packet, and a coin is placed against the front card. It stays there, even when the card is pulled away from behind it; and another card after that. This is explained by stating that the cards have been treated with a newly discovered "slippery mucilage" which makes things stick in one direction, but slide in another. It sounds incredible, yet the demonstration can be continued, card after card.

• **MATERIALS:** Playing cards, adhesive tape, a magnet, and a metal washer.

• **WHAT TO DO:** Tape the magnet to the back of a playing card, beforehand. Show the card with a few others in front of it, keeping the magnet away from view. Place the washer on the front card and the magnet will hold it there, because the washer is magnetic. Say that the washer is held there by a special glue or mucilage, then draw the front card slowly upward, adding that the mucilage is slippery in that direction. The washer stays, still held by the hidden magnet and the process is repeated, card after card.

• **WHAT HAPPENS:** Since the magnet holds the washer, it naturally stays in place when the card is drawn straight upward. By drawing *up* instead of *down*, there is no chance of the washer shaking loose.

• **REMARKS:** By cutting out the centres of some old playing cards and sticking the edges together—with real mucilage, not the "slippery" kind!—you can make a shallow box in which to hide the magnet, with a card pasted in front and another behind. This should be no thicker than half a pack, so by adding a half-pack of loose cards, you will have what appears to be a normal pack with the magnet hidden within it.

Put a few cards in front and you can proceed with the "Slippery Mucilage" demonstration with no fear of detection. Instead of steel washers certain bottle caps may be used, or even paper clips.

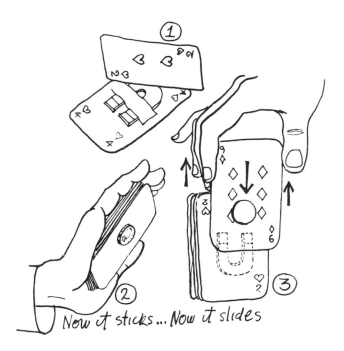

Now it sticks... Now it slides

The Suction Cup

• **EFFECT:** A paper drinking cup is set on the flat blade of a table knife. One hand is placed on top of the cup, with the statement that this will create suction. The other hand turns over the knife, the first hand moves away and the cup remains mysteriously suspended from the blade. The free hand finally removes the inverted cup and both the cup and knife can be given for examination.

• **MATERIALS:** A paper drinking cup, a table knife with a steel blade, and a small segment of a narrow magnet.

• **WHAT TO DO:** Beforehand, drop the magnet in the paper cup. To perform, pick up the cup without showing its interior and set it upright on the blade of the knife, which is held by the other hand. The magnet is attracted to the blade, but you place your free hand over the cup, pretending to "create suction." Invert the knife and cup, with the hand still in place, then move the hand away. The cup remains attached to the blade. When you bring your free hand up beneath the cup and grip the rim with thumb and fingers, you can lift the knife and the magnet will drop into your lower hand. Cup and knife can be given for inspection while you secretly pocket the tiny magnet.

• **WHAT HAPPENS:** The magnetic force works through the bottom of the cup, holding the magnet to the knife blade. When you grip the cup and lift the blade the magnet is blocked by the intervening bottom of the cup and naturally falls unnoticed as described.

• **REMARKS:** Mention of "suction" is simply a bluff. You pretend that you are using one scientific principle in order to disguise the one that is actually responsible for the trick.

CREATE "SUCTION"

Turn over & LET GO!

Magnet in paper cup

Geometrix

Tricks Involving
Geometrical Principles

Deep in the Heart of Texas

- **EFFECT:** The "Heart of Texas" should be its very centre, but due to the state's irregular shape, it seems impossible to determine exactly where that centre is. Yet with a cut-out map of Texas and a few minor items, you can surprise everyone by showing them the geographical centre of the state.
- **MATERIALS:** A cardboard cut-out traced from a map of Texas. A push-pin, a thin string, a weight, such as a fish-weight, or a metal nut or washer. A pencil and a ruler.
- **WHAT TO DO:** Push the pin through a spot "A" near one edge of the map. Attach the string and weight to the pin, then fix it to the wall, so that the cardboard map dangles freely. Trace this line with pencil and ruler. Next, hang the map from another point, "B," and trace that line. Where the lines cross is the centre of the state; but to verify it further, hang the map from another point, "C," and trace the third line to make sure that all converge.
- **WHAT HAPPENS:** The cross-lines, "A," "B," "C," determine the centre of gravity, which is sure to be somewhere along each plumb-line. Finding it by their convergence is a matter of triangulation, as used by surveyors. Fire rangers also use it to sight smoke and mark a line along a map in one fire tower; then sight the same smoke from another tower and check the crossing.

- **REMARKS:** This same test may be made with a map of any other state, country, or island, and will give the same result.

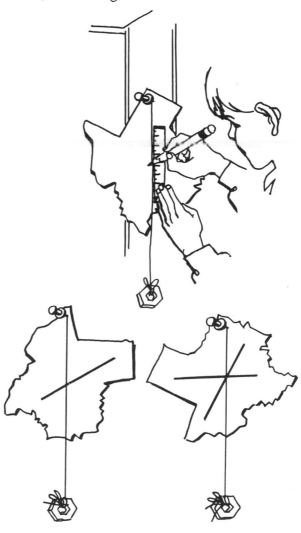

107

The Impossible Loop

- **EFFECT:** A long strip of newspaper is formed into a loop, which should naturally have two edges and also two sides—outside and inside. But this loop has only one edge and even more remarkable, it has only one side, as can be proved by drawing a continuous line along its centre, back to the starting point!
- **MATERIALS:** A double spread from a full-sized newspaper, a pair of scissors, paste or mending tape, and a red pencil or crayon.

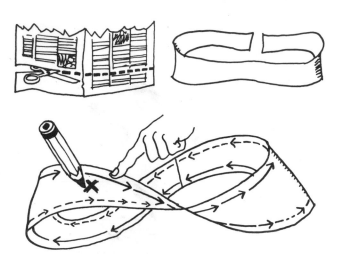

- **WHAT TO DO:** Cut a crosswise strip four inches or more in width from the double page of the newspaper. Form this into a loop and hold it while you point out that it has two edges and two sides. Lower one end and bring it up in place again, giving it a half-twist before pasting or taping it to the other end.

That done, you can show that the loop has only one edge. Start at any spot, make a red mark, and run your finger along the edge. As observers watch, they will be surprised to see your finger arrive back at the mark. Next, take the red pencil and draw a solid line down the centre of the loop.

Amazingly, this too, comes back to the starting point.

- **WHAT HAPPENS:** The twist produces unusual geometric conditions with equally puzzling results. This was first noted by a famous German mathematician, Mobius, a century and a half ago. A surface twisted in the manner described has therefore become known as a "Mobius sheet" or "strip."

The Double Loop

- **EFFECT:** A long loop is formed from a strip of newspaper. The loop is cut along its centre, so everyone expects it to fall into two loops of equal size, but only half the original width. Instead, it turns out to be a half-width loop of double the original diameter!
- **MATERIALS:** A double sheet of newspaper, scissors, paste or mending tape. A pencil may also be used.
- **WHAT TO DO:** Cut a strip from the newspaper, give it a half-twist and paste the ends together. Cut along the centre and the double loop will result automatically.
- **WHAT HAPPENS:** The half-twist turns the

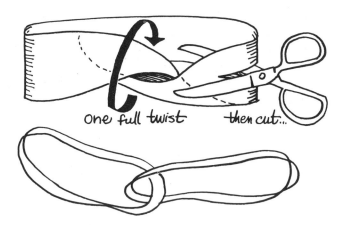

one full twist   then cut...

loop into a "Mobius Strip" with only one side and one edge. When this geometric oddity is cut lengthwise along the centre, it still winds up with only one edge and one side—not having any more to start—so it naturally doubles in size.

• **REMARKS:** This experiment can be preceded by a demonstration of "The Impossible Loop" (page 108) which explains the peculiarity of the "Mobius sheet." Afterward, a finger can be run along the edge of the double loop and a red line drawn up its centre to show that it still conforms to the conditions noted by Professor Mobius, its famous discoverer.

Or, if preferred, the twisted loop may be made up beforehand and simply cut as if it were an ordinary loop of paper, thus baffling everyone completely.

Loop the Loop

• **EFFECT:** A long loop of paper is cut along its centre so that it forms two separate loops of half the original width. Nothing remarkable about that, except that the two loops happen to be linked. That should be impossible; but there it is!

• **MATERIALS:** A double sheet of newspaper, scissors, paste or mending tape.

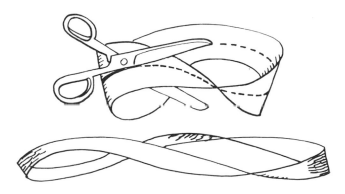

• **WHAT TO DO:** Cut a cross-strip from the double sheet, making it 4 inches in width or more. Give one end of the strip a full twist before pasting or taping it to the other. Cut along the centre and the result will be two loops, linked together.

• **WHAT HAPPENS:** The double twist conforms to the principle of the "Mobius Strip" which has only one side and one edge to start, but winds up as described, producing another geometric surprise. This time there are two loops, but each with only one edge and one side, proving that Professor Mobius was right.

• **REMARKS:** This can well be preceded by "The Double Loop" (page 108) as further demonstration of what can happen with the "Mobius sheet." But rather than get into technicalities, it may be better to prepare the double-twisted or full-twisted loop beforehand and let people try to figure it out for themselves.

The Knot That Is Not

• **EFFECT:** A piece of string is knotted around a short cardboard tube. The knot is then inserted in the tube. The ends of the string are drawn taut and the tube is taken away. The knot, in some surprising way, has dissolved and is gone.

• **MATERIALS:** A piece of string and a short tube rolled from a piece of cardboard, or cut from a mailing tube. The exact length can be determined by experiment.

• **WHAT TO DO:** Tie a simple knot around the outside of the tube, so that one end carries off to the right. Push that end through the tube from the right, tilting the tube slightly so the end slides downward. Then draw the knot off to the right and stuff it into the tube. Let someone hold the ends of the string and pull them taut while you slide the tube along the string. When the tube is removed, the knot will be gone.

• **WHAT HAPPENS:** A simple knot can be un-

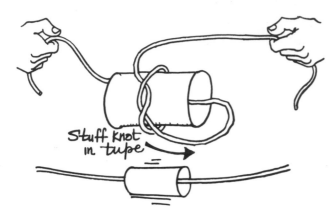

tied by merely pushing its end back through it. That is done in this case, but the knot happens to be tied around the tube when the end goes back through. Removing the string from around the tube thereby disposes of the knot, but that is not apparent until the tube is moved away, and by then it seems quite magical.

The Lost Line

• **EFFECT:** A sheet of paper is marked with nine upright lines, which anyone can count. But when they look again, there are only eight. One line has mysteriously lost itself.

• **MATERIALS:** A sheet of paper marked with nine heavy lines, cut diagonally from upper left to lower right, as in Fig. 1.

• **WHAT TO DO:** Hold the paper by opposite corners—upper left and lower right—and let people count nine complete lines. (Fig. 1) Turn the paper away for a moment and in so doing, draw the upper section diagonally upward, a space of one line to the left. You can then show that there are only eight lines. (Fig. 2)

• **WHAT HAPPENS:** The extra line is not "lost." Instead, the equivalent of one line is added to others, each receiving a proportionate segment. The result is eight lines instead of nine, but all are longer than at the start.

• **REMARKS:** This experiment can be per-

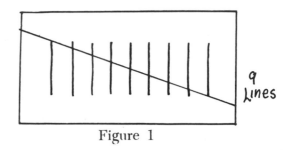

Figure 1

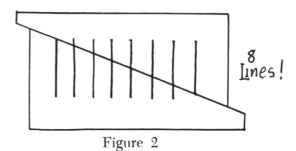

Figure 2

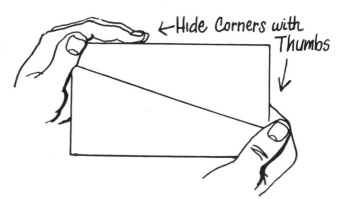

formed with the two portions of the paper lying on the table, but in that case, the pointed corners will show after the halves are shifted diagonally. By holding the corners with thumbs above, fingers below, you change nine lines into eight, without revealing the telltale corners. You can then reverse the shift, changing eight lines back to nine. The paper will then be a perfect rectangle when you lay it on the table. This adds to the mystery.

It Shall Knot Pass

• **EFFECT:** A string is tied in a firm double knot, with a small loop below. A ring is placed on one end of the string and another double knot is tied above the ring. The ends of the string are held by someone, and a

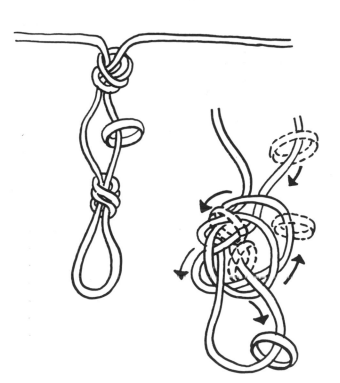

handkerchief is thrown over all. The demonstrator reaches beneath the cloth and mysteriously transfers the ring from the upper loop to the lower.

• **MATERIALS:** A fairly long string, a finger ring, and a handkerchief.

• **WHAT TO DO:** Beneath the cloth, loosen the knot between the loops. Slide the ring downward along the string, through the opened knots, to the loop beneath. Pull the knots tight again and remove the handkerchief to show the surprising result.

• **WHAT HAPPENS:** Actually, it is physically impossible to draw a solid finger ring through an equally solid knot. But when the ring is on the string, and the string itself runs through the knot, it is merely a case of carrying the ring along the string, which you do by loosening the string sufficiently.

The Vanishing Domino

• **EFFECT:** Three pieces of cardboard are arranged to show a drawing of thirteen dominoes, forming a column as in Fig. A. By simply shifting two of the cardboard pieces, one of the dominoes vanishes, leaving only twelve as shown in Fig. B.

• **MATERIALS:** A tracing of the diagram in Fig. A, which can be transferred to a sheet of cardboard with the aid of carbon paper. When cut along the marked lines, it forms three pieces.

• **WHAT TO DO:** Arrange the three pieces as in Fig. A, and the column will contain thirteen dominoes. After people count these, you transpose the two pieces at the right, forming Fig. B, and the count automatically will be reduced to twelve.

• **WHAT HAPPENS:** This is simply a variation

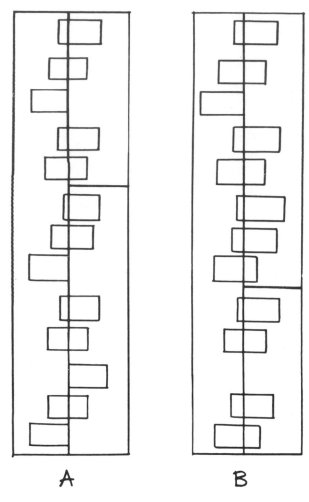

A   **B**

these are arranged in rectangular form, the squares total 65. Somehow an extra square has arrived from nowhere!

- **MATERIALS:** A sheet of stiff paper on cardboard ruled into an 8 × 7 square. A pair of scissors.
- **WHAT TO DO:** Make an exact copy of the 8 x 8 square shown in Fig. 1. Cut this into four pieces, as shown in Fig. 1-A. Lay out the 8 x 8 square and let people count its smaller squares, a total of 64. Separate the pieces and rearrange them as shown in Fig. 2-A. The rectangle will then be 5 x 13, giving a total of 65 squares, which can be counted by anyone. This is shown in Fig. 2.

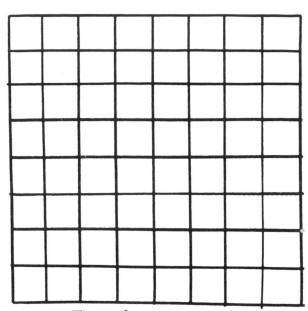

Figure 1

of the "Lost Line," with drawings of dominoes being used instead of simple lines. Also, the dominoes appear in diagonal form, so that the diagram can be cut straight across and down, instead of diagonally. Note, too, that the dominoes are set in groups, rather than in a single row or column. All this helps to disguise the principle involved, making the trick puzzling even to people who are familiar with the simpler version.

The Square That Wasn't There

- **EFFECT:** A square diagram composed of 64 squares is cut into four sections. When

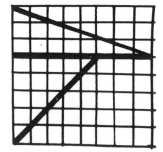

Figure 1A

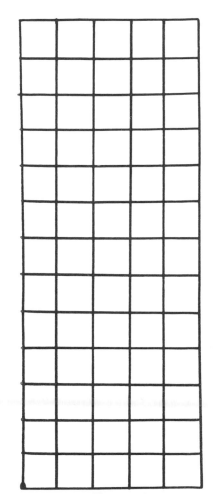

Figure 2A

Figure 2

left there. This is repeated with other coins, but each coin must start from an empty circle and finish on one that is unoccupied. After seven coins have been pushed to circles, an eighth coin is laid on the circle that is still vacant.

This looks easy to do, but when people try it, they are very apt to fail. However, anyone who knows the secret can do it so rapidly that observers are unable to follow the moves.

• **MATERIALS:** A copy of the chart. Eight small coins. Checkers or buttons will also do.

• **WHAT TO DO:** Start from any circle and move to another (as A to D), but place the next coin on a circle from which it can be moved to the one you just left. (In this case, F to A.) Continue thus until you have moved seven coins; then place the eighth on the one remaining circle.

Example: A to D, F to A, C to F, H to C, E to H, B to E, G to B, place coin on G.

• **WHAT HAPPENS:** An interesting geometric principle is involved here. Study the diagram and you will note that each circle represents the focal point for two others. Thus A, for example, provides direct lines to D and F,

• **WHAT HAPPENS:** Actually, the arrangement shown in Fig. 2 is not a perfect rectangle. There are some slight irregularities resulting from the cuts, which add up to almost the equivalent of one square, thus raising the actual total of 64 to an apparent 65. The pieces fit so closely that the average person will think they are exact.

Push Along Coins

• **EFFECT:** Using a chart like the one shown here, a coin is placed on a circle and pushed along a straight line to another circle and

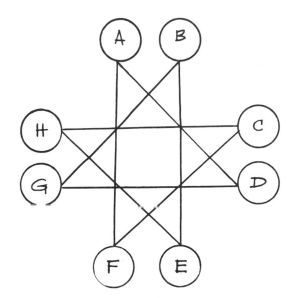

either way. Hence using A as a starting point (as A to D) means that it must be used as a finish for the other line (F to A). By thus disposing of each circle in turn and following the rule throughout, the experiment becomes automatic.

The Impossible Knot

• **Effect:** Someone is given a length of rope and is asked to tie a knot in the centre without releasing one end. After that proves to be impossible, you take the rope and proceed to do it!

• **Materials:** A piece of rope about 24 inches long. A heavy string of the same length will do.

• **What To Do:** Let people take the ends of the rope and try to tie a knot without result. When your turn comes, stretch the rope along the edge of a table. Then fold

your arms, stoop and take one end of the rope in each hand. Unfold your arms and show a knot in the middle of the rope.

• **What Happens:** In folding your arms, you actually tie them in a knot. When you grip the ends of the rope, it becomes an extension of your arms. In unfolding your arms, you transfer the knot to the rope, completing a very neat scientific experiment.

Hypnotrix

Feats of Pretended Hypnotism

Hypnotic Breeze

- **EFFECT:** A person is told to hold his hand straight out, with thumb upward. The demonstrator reaches in the air, snaps his fingers, and points them straight at the person's palm. To his amazement, the person feels a breeze emanating from the performer's fingertips, seemingly a case of hynotic control.
- **WHAT TO DO:** Snap your fingers, then bring them all together, swing your hand downward with a long sweep and stop abruptly, with your fingers pointing directly at the subject's palm, your thumb being upward. He will feel the breeze, for it arrives automatically.
- **WHAT HAPPENS:** It is simply an experiment with air currents, though few people ever suspect it. The snapping is all for effect, merely to make people think you are gathering some etheric force from the atmosphere, though you are doing nothing of the sort.

What you really do is to create an actual breeze by the downsweep of your hand, with your fingers held together. By stopping with your fingers pointing straight toward the subject's palm, you divert the breeze his way and he feels it as a cross-current, which comes along your hand and seems to issue from your fingertips.

Head and Foot

- **EFFECT:** A person is asked to stoop forward and press the top of his head against the wall of the room while he measures off three foot-lengths and brings his feet together keeping them there. He is then told that he cannot move without using his hands to press against the wall, and to his surprise he finds that he is totally helpless.
- **WHAT TO DO:** Have the person place the tip of his right foot against the wall; then the tip of his left foot against the heel of his right. At the same time, he is to lean forward, so the top of his head contacts the wall; then, tell him to put the toe of his right foot against the heel of his left. Following that, he is to bring back his left foot so it is alongside his right.

Now, tell him that if he keeps his feet together and puts his hands behind his back, he will be hypnotized to the point where he is helpless. When he follows your suggestion, he finds that you are right. He just can't budge.

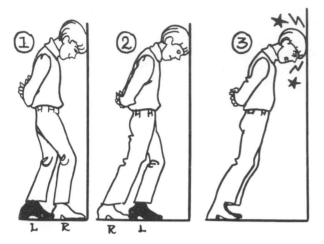

• **WHAT HAPPENS:** Naturally, no hypnotism is involved. It is simply an experiment in balance. When the person puts his left foot behind his right, he still has his balance; but when he puts his right behind his left and stoops forward, his balance is maintained by his head and his left foot. Withdrawing his left foot and bringing it back beside his right means that his support is divided between his head and his right foot, which is too great a span for him to regain his balance.

Hypnotic Fingers

• **EFFECT:** A person is told to place two fingers tip to tip. He is then told to double his other fingers and press their knuckles together. He is then told to separate his extended fingertips—if he can—but when he tries, he finds them to be helpless, as though they were hypnotized.

• **WHAT TO DO:** Have someone place the tips of his forefingers togethers, then double the knuckles of his other fingers. Demonstrate this yourself and show how easily the forefingers can be separated. Do the same with your second fingers, doubling the rest, and have your subject copy the action. Again, the extended fingers separate easily.

Now, press the tips of your third fingers together, double the rest, and tell your subject to do the same. Immediately separate your hands and make "hypnotic" passes at the subject's hands, telling him his fingers are now powerless. To his amazement, he just can't move those third fingers at all.

• **WHAT HAPPENS:** The muscles of the third fingers are weaker than the others. Once they are pressed tip to tip, with the other fingers doubled, it is impossible to separate them. You show how easy it is with the first two fingers, but in coming to the third, you leave the subject pressing his fingertips together (as shown below) and make "hypnotic" passes to prove that he cannot lift them apart.

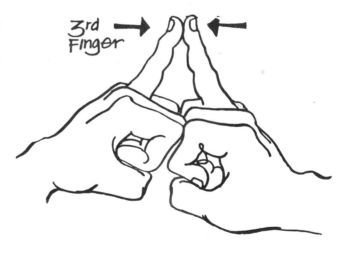

The Hypnotized Knee

• **EFFECT:** A person is told to stand with his feet about six or eight inches apart. You

make hypnotic passes toward his left knee; then tell him to try to lift his left foot straight upward. To his surprise, he can't; seemingly, his left knee has become helpless.

• **WHAT TO DO:** In showing your "subject" how you want him to stand, place him so his right shoulder is against the wall. Then have him move his left foot a few inches to the left; his right foot to the right. This brings his right foot against the wall, though his stance is natural and he is equally balanced on both feet.

Make your hypnotic passes toward his left knee, then say, "Try to lift your left foot straight up!" From his present position it will be impossible. Before he can guess why, tell him move a few paces, then try again. He will be surprised anew to find his knee is suddenly back in action.

• **WHAT HAPPENS:** When standing with both feet several inches apart, any attempt to raise one foot means that the weight must be shifted entirely to the other. To do that, the person must lean well to the right, so that his right shoulder will counterbalance his left foot. Since he is standing with his right shoulder against the wall, such a shift is impossible. Try it yourself and you will find that your left foot tries to respond, but your left knee won't. So when you work it on a friend, tell him that you've hypnotized his knee.

The Rising Arms

• **EFFECT:** A person is told to watch your arms and that when you raise them, his arms will rise, too. Almost in spite of himself, his arms rise at your command, as though hypnotized.

• **WHAT TO DO:** After stating what you intend to do, tell the person to stand in a doorway and press his arms outward and upward against the sides of the doorway.

Add that he is to keep pressing as hard as he can, since the doorway will prevent his arms from rising higher.

Then tell him to keep watching your eyes and that when you count to ten, you want him to walk toward you. When you reach "Ten," you raise your own arms from your side and as he steps forward, his arms come upward just like yours.

• **WHAT HAPPENS:** Steady pressure of his arms against the doorway produces a muscular reaction. Once clear of the door, the person's arms rise automatically because of the continued pressure. Try this beforehand yourself and you will learn how surprising the result can be. When you work the experiment with a friend, many onlookers will think you really hypnotized his arms.

A Hypnotic Touch

• **EFFECT:** A person seated in a chair is asked to stretch backward, fold his arms, and extend his feet. By simply pressing a fingertip against his forehead, you can prevent him from rising from the chair.

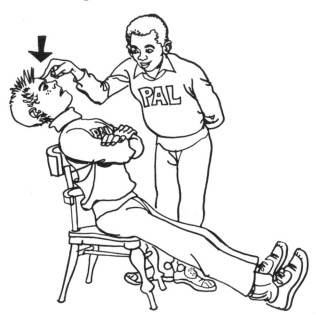

• **WHAT TO DO:** Make sure of the person's exact position. He must have his feet well extended and his head far back. You remind him that he is to keep his arms folded; then say: "Try to rise straight up from your chair! You will be unable to do so! You will be powerless to rise until I say you can!"

After he has struggled helplessly, relax the downward pressure of your finger and announce: "Now, you can rise!" To his amazement, he will find that he can rise after all.

• **WHAT HAPPENS:** Since your "subject" has his feet extended, he must first raise his head in order to gain sufficient balance to rise from the chair. Steady pressure of your forefinger against the centre of his forehead prevents him from raising his head and thereby holds him helpless. When you relax pressure, he naturally can rise.

The Brush-Off

• **EFFECT:** You stroke a person's sleeve with a hairbrush three times and ask: "How many times did you feel the brush?" He says, "Three." So you brush his shoulder twice and ask the same question, to which he responds, "Two." Finally, you brush his back five times and ask: "How many time did you feel the brush?" He replies, "Five times," but when you turn to other people and ask if he is right, they all say, "No! You only brushed his back four times." When you tell your victim that you hypnotized him into thinking that you gave him an extra brush stroke, he will be ready to believe you.

• **MATERIALS:** A hairbrush, or a similar brush, with fairly soft bristles.

• **WHAT TO DO:** Brush the person's arm three times with the brush; then do the same with his shoulder, twice, so he can see what happens. Then brush his back with four long, downward sweeps, pausing momentarily between them. After the fourth time, transfer the brush to your left hand and stroke the back of his coat with your right hand instead of the brush. When you ask, "How many times did you feel the brush?" he is almost sure to say, "Five," only to have eyewitnesses tell him he is wrong.

• **What Happens:** A person's arm or shoulder may be sensitive enough to distinguish between brush strokes and hand strokes; but his back is less so. Add the fact that he cannot see what you are doing, but has reached the point where he takes it for granted, and the fact that he gives the wrong answer is not suprising—except to himself. Hypnotists sometimes use this experiment to show how easily people respond to false suggestions.

• **What To Do:** Spread your right hand and clamp it firmly on your head, raising your forearm to a horizontal position. Tell people to grab your arm and pull your hand up. Keep raising your elbow all the time they are trying. They become helpless.

• **What Happens:** In trying to thrust your forearm upward, they bring your upper arm along. Since your arm is attached to your shoulder, they are actually trying to lift your entire body, rather than just your right hand. Even a champion weight-lifter couldn't do that, while thrusting himself upward and off balance.

• **Remarks:** Even a very light person can work this effectively, as the lifter is at a total disadvantage. Instead of pressing your hand on your head, you can just use your extended fingertips, but the result will be the same; in fact, even better, as you will be pressing downward from a slightly higher elevation.

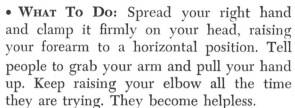

The Heavy Hand

• **Effect:** One person clamps his hand hard upon his head and invites others to try to pull his hand upward. They strain and struggle, but find it impossible. This is attributed to hypnotic power.